SICILY

A Heart's Journey

Library of Congress Control Number: 2018955359

Sicily. A Heart's Journey by Mary Tolaro Noyes
ISBN 978-1-939693-32-7

Other Publications by Mary Tolaro Noyes:

In English

Bologna Reflections: An Uncommon Guide
Gathering Chestnuts: Encounters Along The Way
Travelers Tales San Francisco: Dreaming of Muir Woods
30 Days in Italy: The Gift
A Woman's World Again: Leila's Gesture

In Italian

Sicilia: Un Viaggio Verso le Radici – the Italian version of this book
Gente di Gaggio, #29: Con Clara nel castagneto
La Mùsola, #58: Come se fossimo in paradiso
Nuèter, #65: Le "tigelle" della zia
Emilia Romagna Segreta: Bologna Enigmatica
I segreti della cucina dell'Emilia Romagna: Bologna: The Cooking Show
Racconti Bolognesi, Vol II: I segreti di Bologna, città seducente
Racconti Emiliani: Nel castagneto con Clara

For information and for orders, write to:

Legas

P. O. Box 149
Mineola, New York
11501, USA

3 Wood Aster Bay
Ottawa, Ontario
K2R 1D3 Canada

Legaspublishing.com

Mary Tolaro Noyes

SICILY

A Heart's Journey

LEGAS

Acknowledgements

Special thanks to my husband Tom Noyes for his assistance and support because *Sicily: A Heart's Journey* could not exist without his collaboration. I dedicate *Sicily: A Heart's Journey* to my paternal grandparents, Filippo Tolaro and Maria Calogera Zarba; to my parents Philip Tolaro and Rita Thibodeaux Tolaro; to my American aunts, uncles and cousins, sisters and brother; and to the Sicilian Tolaro and Zarba families, whose welcome helped to make the journey possible. I offer special thanks to the American family members who have over the years joined me in reconnecting our American and Sicilian families: our sons T. James and Philip Noyes, niece Melissa Wagoner Olesen, cousins Jeanine Carr, Matthew and Michelle Raymond, and Julius and Gloria Tolaro. Special thanks to Bruna Bruni O'Neall, my first Italian teacher, who helped me write the letters that reached the family in 1989 and this story to unfold. Likewise, I offer sincere gratitude to Father Giovanni Bongiovanni, the pastor of Santa Maria di Gesù Parish, who received one of the original letters and tracked down my Pietrini relatives. Thank you also to Sig. Giuseppe Maddelena, for his wonderful photos; the *Biblioteca Comunale di Pietraperzia*; and the town of Pietraperzia. Thank you to the *Historical Society of Bellows Falls, Vermont*; the *Historical Society of North Walpole, New Hampshire*; the *Rockingham Free Public Library*; and the *Boston and Maine Railroad Historical Society*. Thank you to Arba Sicula and to Professor Gaetano Cipolla. Lastly, thank you to my family, in both the United States and Italy. My heart is filled with love and gratitude.

For:

Tom

In Memory of:

Maria Calogera Zarba

Filippo Tolaro

Philip William Tolaro

Rita Thibodeaux Tolaro

Maria Calogera Zarba

Filippo Tolaro

Figure 1. Maria and Filippo, early 1920s

Contents

Preface

The collection of stories in *Sicily: A Heart's Journey* chronicles the dream of discovering my Sicilian family—from its origin as a child surrounded by the love of my family, to its realization on a June day in 1989. My story, like so many others, reveals the power of family love that transcends time and place and enriches the lives of each generation. My father's lifelong search to find his extended family became mine. I will be forever grateful to him for this and for the joy we experienced together in accomplishing the dream—together and with the help of many other family members on both sides of the ocean.

Figure 2. Dad with Zio Rocco picking grapes, June 1992

About the Author

Mary Tolaro Noyes was raised in Bellows Falls, Vermont, across the Connecticut River from North Walpole, New Hampshire, where her Sicilian grandparents settled in 1913. She and her husband Tom now live in Oakland, California. Motivated by rediscovering her grandparents' families in Sicily in 1989, she studied Italian, mostly in Bologna, Italy, in order to be able to communicate with the family in Pietraperzia. Since 1989 she has spent a significant amount of time with them and journeyed extensively around the island. She and her husband Tom were able to accompany her parents there three times and witness the joy that a reunion can offer to so many individuals. Perhaps discovering that her grandparents' love story was not just a fairytale, but a real love story has been greatest reward of the journey. Her indispensible companion along the way has always been her husband Tom Noyes.

Figure 3. Author Mary with her husband, Tom - 30th anniversary, 2000

Tolaro Cast of Characters

Filippo Tolaro
  Father: Giuseppe Tolaro
  Mother: Maria Calogera Torrenti

First cousins of my grandfather Filippo Tolaro in Pietraperzia
in 1989

<u>Giuseppe</u> – Rosaria (Sara) Bongiovanni
          Salvatore – Ornella Carrara
          Nina Tolaro – Rocco Messina
          Maria Gina – Filippo Miccichè

<u>Giovanni</u> – Giacoma Russo
          Salvatore (Totò)
          Antonella (Nina) – Rocco Pagliaro
                    Pagliaro Francesca –Vincenzo Zarba
                    Pagliaro Giacoma – Filippo Puzzo
                    Pagliaro Emanuele
                    Pagliaro Letizia

<u>Paolo</u> (had recently passed away) – Angelina Zuccalà
          Salvatore (Totò) – Lina Fiaccaprile
                    Paolo
                    Fabrizio
          Calogero

Zarba Cast of Characters

Maria Calogera Zarba
 Father: Vincenzo Zarba
 Mother: Damiana Mulara

Sisters:
Giuseppina – Lo Manto Antonino
 Lo Manto Dora – Salvatore Monella (Montreal)
  Monella Joseph
 Lo Manto Damiana – Bifarella Calogero
  Bifarella Rosario (Montreal)
  Bifarella Antonino -- Dina
  Bifarella Concetta – Angelo Farina
  Bifarella Giuseppe (Montreal)
 Lo Manto Giovanni (Milan)
 Lo Manto Enzo (Montreal)
 Lo Manto Giuseppe (Torino)
 Lo Manto Josi (Torino)
 Lo Manto Ninetta – Armando Blandino (Montreal)

Francesca – Died at age 30

Brothers:
Giovanni – Family in Argentina
Rocco – Paola Puzzo
 Vincenzo – Tommasina (Masina) Amico
  Ausilia
  Roberto
 Rosario – Graziella Di Maggio
  Rocco
  Frediana
  Nicangelo
 Calogero (Lillo) – Maria Puzzo
  Massimo
  Paola
  Vincenzo

Damiana – Filippo Valverdi
    Valverdi Michele
    Valverdi Roberto
    Valverdi Fabrizio
    Valverdi Claudio

<u>Salvatore</u> – Concetta Giunta
  Vincenzo – Filippina Vinci
      Maria – Giuseppe Milazzo
      Concetta – Salvatore Bellomo
      Lidia
  Antonietta – Calogero Barrile
      Barrile Salvatore
      Barrile Concetta – Salvatore Marotta
         Marotta Daniela
         Marotta Giuseppe
      Barrile Filippo
  Giacomo – Rosetta Romano
      Marisa
      Rosalba
  Francesco – Mirella

American Cast of Characters

Family of Filippo Tolaro and Maria Calogera Zarba

Joseph (1914-08-27) – Rae Stevens
Mary (1916-02-11) – Joseph La Torre
   Philip La Torre – Marianne Lightbody
         Laina
   Ellen La Torre – Jerry Totten
James (1918-03-16) – Margaret Kane
              – Catherine Collins
Philip (1920-07-25) – Rita Thibodeaux
   Mary Alice – Thomas Noyes
        T. James Noyes – Karen Tosti
        Philip Noyes – Angela Major
   Terry Ann – William Wagoner
        Melissa Ann – Peter Olesen
        Emily Marie – Richard Holt
   Philip
   Rita Lynn – Curtis Webb
        Robert Keim
        Jamie Keim – Kelsea Beig
Anna (1922-10-08) – Clayton Raymond
   Lawrence Raymond – Marilyn Martin
        Kelly DeForest
        Anna Raymond
        Matthew Raymond – Michelle Raymond
Michael (1924-08-20) –Jennifer Johnson
   Michael Doty Tolaro – Ron Doty Tolaro
        Jennifer Tolaro – Timothy Heidbrink
   Linda Tolaro – Bill Striegel
        Elizabeth Striegel
Gloria (1928-04-22) – James Carr
   Jeanine Carr
   James Carr – Alice Huggins
        Emilie Carr – Seth Smeltz
Frances (1934-08-29) – Phillip Crosby

Sicily: A Heart's Journey

Where is Pietraperzia?

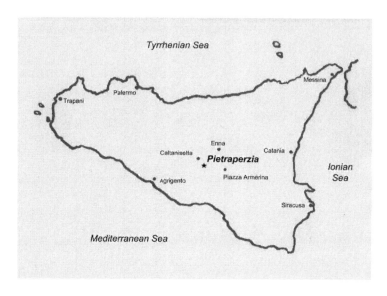

Figure 4. Map of Sicily with Pietraperzia highlighted

Figure 5. Mountains North of Enna, Sicily

Journey

*Life is the journey and **Sicily: A Heart's Journey** is just one of the distant mountains.*

It's like the mountains I saw marching ridge

After ridge into the distant horizon. The gauzy

Air hung velvet-heavy between us, each succeeding

Green or rocky crest more faded from view than the

Next. But in the mystery flamed the desire to see

Beyond, to clarify the image, to sharpen the amorphous

Vision, discovering that hunger always returns, will

Never be tamed once and forever: The journey,

Conquering one ridge, only assures a closer

Glimpse of future possibilities beyond yesterday

And today, the promise of tomorrow.

Figure 6. New Hampshire, across Connecticut River, from Bellows Falls

Figure 7. Bellows Falls, seen from Table Rock, N. Walpole, c. 1970s

Prologue

"I'm sorry, Papà, but Filippo is my husband now, and I will go with him, wherever he goes." With that, Maria Calogera turned away, and left her family's home in Pietraperzia, Sicily, forever. That was in November 1913. As her American granddaughter growing up in a small Vermont town with my Sicilian-American family close by, I heard their love story often: she would hold me on her lap and recount the fairytale about her Prince Charming, my grandfather Filippo Tolaro, their courtship, marriage, and life in America.

Figure 8. Pietraperzia, Villa Tortorici

My connection to the country of my Sicilian grandparents has always been strong. Perhaps because of my grandmother's stories, Sicily and Italy were places in my own fairytale, a little like our wonderfully chaotic family gatherings at my grandparents' home in North Walpole, New Hampshire, and the memories of extended family get-togethers at Aunt Mary and Uncle Joe's house in East Boston. Excursions to Boston's North End with my grandparents, uncle, and father come alive when I think back to the aroma of baking bread along the streets and my very first taste of *granita al limone*, made in the old fashioned, street side style.

This collection of stories grew out of that childhood in a small southern Vermont village and my grandparents' home just across the Connecticut River. I was the oldest of four children, in a family whose world revolved around those paternal grandparents, the abundant aunts, uncles, and cousins, and each other. Family always came first. I grew up believing, at least just a little, that Italy's reputation in the world depended on me. I was proud to be Italian: I had to behave and do my best because I had a responsibility not only to myself and to my family, but yes, to all of Italy.

My father Philip always instilled in us four children the love and importance of family. Italy and Sicily in particular set the backdrop for our childhood world, even though we were in a very American small town in Vermont. Together with my mother Rita, he not only taught us with his words, but also with the way he lived his life, that knowing and understanding where we came from would enrich our lives. For this reason, we were very fortunate to connect with our extended Tolaro family and that of our Thibodeaux mother. My parents made sure that we knew cousins, aunts and uncles, and grandparents and established relationships with them. My father's insistence grew out of his closeness to his own sisters and brothers, but also out of his lifelong yearning to know his cousins, any that might have been in the United States and Canada, but also in Sicily. He passed on his dream to me.

Before my first trip to that imagined wonderland, Italy was the shivers I felt when I heard but did not understand the lovely language.

Figure 9. Filippo working on the railroad, c. 1930

It was dancing to the songs that my grandmother had hummed while the old "Victrola" played. We would sway and hop in circles together in the living room. After her death, Italy became my sweet memories and the longing to understand her better and connect with her origins, and mine. It was flashy articles in travel magazines and nebulous plans to one day learn Italian, find my family, and begin the pilgrimage.

It happened in 1989. The plans were made, which included my learning a little Italian. I did. (Too little, as it turned out.) Next I scoured my grandparents' documents and letters and wrote to the parish church in Pietraperzia, Sicily where they were married in 1913. Within a couple of months I had received letters of welcome from both the Tolaro and Zarba families and from Father Bongiovanni, the parish priest who had found them for me. Together with my parents, my husband, and our sons, I experienced the joy of finally connecting, along with the trepidation of reaching to open and to perhaps enter into a relationship with distant family, burdened as it was with past and present uncertainties.

Figure 10. Downtown Bellows Falls, c. 1900s

Figure 11. Grandmother of Filippo, Giuseppe and Giovanni Tolaro, c. 1900

Figure 12. Philip and Mary, Strait of Messina, June 1989

Figure 13. First sight of Sicily, June 1989

Figure 14. Mary with parents, Philip and Rita, Capri, end of May 1989

Sicily Waits

Heavy, dark sky like Noah's hangs there.
Gray land in the gray distance blurry —
As churning waves toss our giant ferry like a toy,
And the frigid wind whips hair and clothes flapping.

Across the Strait of Messina
Sicily waits . . .
Gray land in the gray distance blurry,
Patiently waiting, always patiently waiting.

Alone with moment upon moment as sadness creeps
And crawls its cold fingers around my soul,
Unanswered questions,
Fears churn inside.

Wind, cold, tears, gray land
In the gray distance blurry make
Dream of golden land
Sad.

Suddenly closer gray slides into wheat drab tan.
Sky moving, rearranging the gray
With soft white, blue,
Promise.

From up above arms reach sunlight down —
Shafts piercing gray dark,
Ripping drab away, shooting
Grand shimmering circles
Onto dark somber water and land,
Now slowly golden.

The ferry touches shore,
As sun-lighting day, soul-lifting
Heart joy's rush brings
Warm tears, welcome

Embrace.

Figure 15. Damiana Mulara and Vincenzo Zarba, Maria Calogera's
parents, c. 1900

The Journey Begins

My Journey began with both excitement and trepidation. The first line of this story describes it well. Fortunately, I could not turn back at that moment, so the rest is history, mine and my American and Sicilian Family's, whose presence has nurtured my heart and soul and propelled the journey forward.

Andiamo ... Let's Go!
14 June 1989

If I could have gotten out of it I would have. What seemed an exciting idea at home in California loomed a fearful reality. There we were, my parents and I, at Punta Raisi Airport in Palermo, Sicily, waving goodbye to our tour group as it left for the United States. We instead were about to shed the lazy tag of *turisti* and venture into the world of *la famiglia*. The mystery that lay before us evoked apprehension. The unknown Tolaro and Zarba families were waiting to welcome us to Pietraperzia, the town in central Sicily near Enna, from which my grandparents had emigrated in 1913. What would we find in 1989?

As a child I had often climbed on my grandmother Maria Calogera Zarba's cushiony lap and, while she held me close, listened to stories about our extended Sicilian family; the lively music and folk dances; the pageants and feast days; and most of all, about my grandfather Filippo, their courtship and marriage. Accounts of her difficult life in Sicily and later in New England captivated me and sustained my curiosity from childhood well into adult life. I knew in my heart that I would visit Sicily someday. I wanted to understand my grandmother better—her strength, her love, her pride, and her powerful impact on me.

Letters from both the Tolaro and Zarba families, welcoming the reunion answered my previous inquiry to the pastor of Santa Maria di Gesù, the parish where Filippo and Maria Calogera's marriage documents were registered, in October 1913. I knew then that my heart's journey could begin.

Yes, I was frightfully worried at that moment at Punta Raisi Airport when we said goodbye to our friends. However, with all the courage I could muster, "andiamo" I said to my parents ... "let's go." It was too late to turn back.

But Where is Caltanissetta?

I really cannot say how we managed to find our way to Caltanissetta, a smaller city southeast of Palermo. Problem number one was the van. The rental car agent, a young man in his mid to late twenties, greeted us pleasantly, very businesslike. Dressed in a brown double breasted suit the color of roasted chestnuts, white dress shirt and swirling gold and olive green tie, he smiled and his friendly eyes looked out through horn-rimmed spectacles. He practiced his 'broken' English, which was superior to my 'very broken' Italian, as he explained the situation.

"I would prefer that you wait for the *pulmino* until ten o'clock," he said, "because you should take the new minivan arriving then. The Fiat I have is old and you will be safer in the new Ford," he assured us, searching into our jittery eyes, looking for approbation, as we stood leaning on the counter.

"Va bene," I answered, "that's fine," and I thought how kind it was for him to be concerned. So we waited expectantly until ten. Shortly thereafter dad and I found ourselves in the lot next to a vehicle with room for nine passengers, plus luggage, that stretched the definition of 'mini' to new limits as far as I was concerned. We came to call it the White Whale. The lump in my throat grew to match it, as the parking spot and narrow exit route seemed to shrink proportionately.

I'm in trouble, I thought, as I fumbled with the alarm button and then the key. I remember wishing my dad would offer to drive . . . he didn't. I tucked up and into the huge seat from the tiny space between our monster and its neighbor and, for the first time in my life, I felt like a truck driver, an experience for which I had never yearned. Then the realization of the transmission hit me. I had not driven a car with a standard transmission for at least eighteen years, let alone a truck. Our adventure had begun . . .

Just grasping the steering wheel with both hands at the same time was a Herculean task. I'm sure it was a standard truck size, enormous. A relatively small 5'2" person, I stretched forever just to touch both sides at once. Turning was another matter. It took the strength of a truck driver too. No power steering, of course.

After starting and stalling four times, at last I managed to shift.

Practically sitting on the gear shift to press it down, I slid it into reverse, all the while keeping in mind that other cars were parked barely a breath away and that, if I didn't keep my foot on the clutch, we'd jerk-stall again, no doubt swiping at least one of them. My dad was great. He didn't say a word, probably afraid that I'd turn the assignment over to him without much encouragement.

Somehow it worked. We actually moved backwards slowly, and in control, from the parking spot and into the narrow passage out of the lot. *Shift into first, forward slowly, move cautiously, the next sharp right and a left onto the circle drive that fronted the departure terminal of the airport–whew* I had made it! With relief I stopped the van and dad went to get mom and the luggage. It seemed like we had already traveled miles. We loaded up and started out.

The day was a beauty as we ventured out onto the main road. Giant, dark Mount Pelegrino jutted high up into the clear, intensely blue sky. The heavy traffic became heavier still as we traveled east toward the center of Palermo. Six random rows of cars and trucks in four marked lanes maneuvered deftly and sped impatiently toward everywhere. I felt at a decided disadvantage as I tried to follow lane markings and speed limits. Horns blared as we jerked along and I gingerly accustomed my eye-hand-foot coordination to the intricacies of driving a standard transmission truck.

Then insight smacked me in the middle of an intersection as I tried to correct a wrong turn that had us on our way up into the hills south of Palermo, indeed on our way to Monreale: *In this tank we're bigger than almost anything on the road,* I thought. *I need to change my attitude.* From that moment on I drove like I owned the road, with authority. Positive thoughts like *watch out Sicilia, here I come*, and *make way, this road is mine* propelled us toward our destination.

It worked. When horns blasted, I stood my ground, intimidating the mostly tiny Fiats. I felt like Moses parting the waters as we slipped easily through Palermo east to the autostrada, and then zipped along Sicily's breathtaking northern coast on route A19.

That part of the trip passed uneventfully. At Imera route A19 turned south toward Buonfornello, Villanova and Caltanissetta. We quietly reminisced about the tour we had just enjoyed and wondered about the reception we could expect in Pietraperzia.

Underneath the calm, a nagging concern kept wiggling its way into my mind: where to go after we left the autostrada at the Caltanissetta exit. None of my general maps gave a clear indication of the route we should follow. I had no map of Caltanissetta, where our hotel was located.

About two hours from the airport we exited the autostrada, turning right, hopefully toward our destination. I was forced to find our way as I had observed Arnaldo, our tour bus driver do, over and over again. I stopped the van wherever convenient, while my father shouted from the window to someone passing: "Dov'è Caltanissetta? (Where is Caltanissetta?)"

We approached the first 'guide' as we followed a curvy, steep road that looked like it took us directly away from the city mixed into the hills, quite a distance ahead of us to the left. We had hoped it would be Caltanissetta. Pleased to meet Americans, the man, sixtyish, wore a pair of denim overalls, like my grandpa used to wear, and a red and tan plaid, long-sleeved shirt. He not only had a brother in New York but also had been there himself. He chatted on and on with dad, we surmised about America and his brother and his trip, and finally said yes, we were on the road to Caltanissetta. About all I could get out of their conversation in Italian with a heavy Sicilian accent was that soon we would pass a railroad station on the right, and we would know we were in Caltanissetta. My father might have understood some of our guide's friendly conversation, but not much considering he only had a few words and phrases from overheard discussions between his parents as he grew up. He was very good at shaking his head in agreement and then looking at me to verify what he thought the conversation was about! According to our guide, the Albergo Di Prima would be right there. I could even picture it! Dad agreed, as he hopped back up into the van. Wow, we thought. Did we ever luck out. Needless to say, we were naive . . .

Too many kilometers later, craving reassurance, we searched again for help. We had not encountered any intersections, so I had not made a wrong turn. We really wondered how we could be on our way to anywhere. We had found no sign to Caltanissetta, or to any other city or town. So, as I drove, dad called out the window again to a man driving his miniature truck on the narrow shoulder: "Are we on the road to Caltanissetta."

Figure 16. Antonietta & Calogero Barrile, 1992

The man assured us that yes indeed we were on our way to Caltanissetta, just straight ahead. Marginally reassured, we continued our trip, going up and down countless hills, viewing stupendous scenery on the right and on the left: rolling hills the color of gold, dotted with clusters of dark green trees; brilliant green vineyards climbing up to meet the clear blue sky; old, gray, stone houses and ancient crumbling castles resting here and there. The panoramic views were marvelous we agreed, but after ten or fifteen minutes, the old question still nagged: Where is Caltanissetta?

Forza, Mary, I thought, keeping my concerns to myself, listening while my father extolled shamelessly the beauty of central Sicily and anticipated with joy the coming reunion. Mom was quiet in the back seat, listening, as she usually does, happy for her husband's contentment.

Somehow we arrived in Caltanissetta, in the midst of swirling traffic. Our timing was perfect: mezzogiorno, and everyone was traveling home to eat the day's pranzo and relax. A midday rush hour. Many of the old, cramped, stone streets curved and climbed and went only one way. "Mamma mia" I said. Jerking along in traffic, we needed help, and fast, before the buzzing swarm would carry us along in its dizzy

31

frenzy, probably right out of town again, missing the hotel. We saw neither a railroad station nor the Albergo Di Prima, like we'd been promised. So in the middle of an intersection I stopped the van and dad once again shouted out the window to a young man on his fast, shiny black Vespa: "Where is the Albergo Di Prima?" as we blocked traffic, horns trumpeting all around us. The young man grinned broadly and motioned us forward saying "Prego ... follow me, I'll show you."

So we followed him straight ahead, then around a wide curve bending to the right, and finally, there was Via Kennedy, a one-way street, luckily going our way. With great effort I turned the steering wheel sharply to the right, while our gallant guide left us, waving goodbye, and sped away smiling. A few meters to the left stood the Albergo Di Prima, but I had to drive past to search out parking. I needed a giant spot. However, typical of all the other Italian towns we had been in over the last three weeks, if there was a parking place, it was probably going to be a tiny make-believe one, in other words, illegal. Making my job even more difficult were the whizzing cars flashing by us on all sides, their drivers perturbed at our slow pace. At least four lines of cars squashed themselves into two marked lanes. I imagined us in a huge white elephant trying to glide through hordes of tiny mice scampering this way and that around our gigantic, flat as a pancake, cumbersome feet. I ached to close my eyes and find myself relaxing on the comfy bed in the quiet hotel room.

"Yea!" I said with immense relief when I spotted it. At the very end of the block, like a prayer answered, waited a beautiful wide space, perfect for parking our 'elephant', and we didn't even have to go up on the sidewalk to fit. *Grazie mille, nonna, you must be up there in heaven watching out for us. Nowhere in Italy have I ever seen such a huge legal parking place. Grazie!* My folks and I just sat there in the parked van for a moment, greatly relieved to actually be in Caltanissetta and amazingly, at our hotel. We congratulated ourselves and marveled at the friendly, helpful Sicilian people who had given us smiles and reassurance, even if we still didn't understand the meaning of "just straight ahead."

The Albergo Di Prima

When we entered the hotel, everyone stopped and stared, mouths agape. We presented ourselves to Signor Luigi at the reception desk, with at least as much self-consciousness as determination, but he had already guessed who we were. That was good, because all at once my few months of Italian and the words my dad remembered from his childhood deserted us. *We're going to have to do better than this*, I realized, as we assured the signore that yes, indeed we were the Americani.

Signor Luigi, probably in his mid-thirties, was thin like a fence post, and tall compared to the other gentlemen we had talked with so far. A quiet, soft-spoken man, perhaps a bit excitable, he had black, thinning hair and wore thick, dark-rimmed glasses. He welcomed us while everyone in the lobby continued to gawk. A tall matronly woman dressed in light blue stood behind the desk with Luigi. Examining us were a hotel porter wearing an official looking jacket with broad red and black vertical stripes, a bartender at the tiny bar in the corner near the door, and two or three men standing there, drinking their caffè.

Figure 17. Paolo Tolaro's family, 1989

Perhaps they were thinking, "Why are these Americans here?" But no one spoke. No one even blinked.

After we had registered, I asked Signor Luigi "Please signore, where is the parking lot that was promised in the confirmation letter?" Try to imagine this conversation in my very elementary Italian, and Signor Luigi's trying to be kind version of Sicilian-Italian, including generous hand and arm gestures.

"The parking lot, sì, there is a parking lot right behind the hotel, signora, and you can put your automobile there now," he explained. "Then the porter will carry your bags to your rooms."

"Va bene," I said, but "how do I get to the parking lot?"

"Oh, that will be easy," he assured me with a smile. "You can use the entrance that comes right before the hotel. It has an iron gate that Salvatore will open for you." He motioned with his right hand and bobbed his head in the porter's direction.

"Grazie, signore," I said, "but I have already parked the car down the street past the hotel, so I need to drive it around the block and enter Via Kennedy again, since it goes only one way."

"No, no, signora, that won't be at all necessary. Just back it up from there to the entrance."

"But signore, the traffic is very heavy," I challenged, "I can't back it up the street against traffic now. It's impossible."

Luigi looked at me, his eyes through the thick lenses a combination of disbelief and concern. "Signora," he began reassuringly, "it's easy. It won't be a problem. Please believe me."

My father was standing to my right, and we looked at each other with glazed eyes, not believing our ears. Finally dad said quietly, "What do you think, Mary? Is it possible?"

I had made up my mind though, not to discuss it further with Signor Luigi, since I couldn't speak Italian well enough. I decided to ignore his counsel, smile agreeably, go out to the van and find my way 'around the block', or whatever that meant.

Figure 18. Salvatore Marotta Family and Filippo Barrile, 1989

So I just said to dad "let's go, okay" and we walked toward the door smiling to Luigi, waving goodbye, saying "ci vediamo presto" and laughing to myself *yes, surely we'll see you soon*.

Crossing the street back to the van reaffirmed my decision not to drive in reverse against traffic just then. We didn't have the right of way as pedestrians, we could tell, and dodged the 'flying' cars as we tried to cross quickly. "I hope we can find Via Kennedy again," I said to dad once we got to the other side.

"Me too . . ." he answered.

We were right to worry about finding our way around the block. I drove perhaps for ten to fifteen minutes, always turning to the right, going around curves and up hills, and finally we did somehow arrive back at Via Kennedy. We were relieved, to be sure. Then all at once we noticed what seemed to be a lot of commotion on the corner as we made our sharp right turn.

Standing there, waving us 'home' anxiously, with worried looks melting into delight, were Signor Luigi, the tall woman, Salvatore the porter, the bartender, and one of the men who had been drinking coffee. They all jogged happily beside us on the sidewalk as we traveled slowly in the leftmost lane toward the gate. While Salvatore opened it we waited, pleased to be at the end of that adventure.

Then I saw where I had to drive next.

The very narrow bumpy driveway, composed of rough ancient stones, dropped straight down, and stopped dead at a solid structure of old gold-colored bricks. I didn't see either a parking place, forget the parking lot, or even a place to turn around. The van seemed very large again, and I prayed the brakes functioned well as we sort of slid down ever so slowly. "Lord," said dad quietly, "Where do we park?"

The brakes worked, and at the bottom I looked to the right and there was Salvatore, in a place so small that I couldn't have turned the van around. He motioned us past where he stood, toward a tiny spot in what resembled a shed underneath the hotel. It was filled with cars, many of which looked like they had been resting for eternity, nestled among random chattel piled high. Into the spot we went and stopped barely short of the gray stonewall. Somehow we fit, just as somehow we had found Caltanissetta and the hotel. "A--men" I said as I rested my head on the steering wheel and collapsed for a few seconds.

Salvatore anxiously waited for us to open the doors and get out so that he could begin to unload the luggage. He was a short man, maybe not even as tall as my 5'2", thin and quite old to be a porter. His hair was totally white, but lively brown eyes and a timid smile made us feel very welcome indeed.

Since the door into the hotel was a distance away, poor Salvatore would have to carry the baggage from the van to the foot of the steep hill we had just descended, up the hill, left at the top toward the veranda, up its many steps, into the lobby where Luigi was again standing at the reception desk, and finally across the lobby to the small elevator. I looked with disbelief at my parents as we all said at once "this poor man has to carry all our bags, probably twelve in number, by himself that distance?"

"Let's help him" mom said quickly.

Salvatore insisted that he could do it himself, but we helped anyway, with him in command. That gentle man was the fastest of us all, and in no time we were ready to cram the pile into the elevator. After three trips up and back down, we finally got the luggage to the third floor and our rooms. We bid Salvatore goodbye with profuse thanks and a tip, and he left us with a shy "di niente." We didn't realize it then, of course, but he became one of our guardian angels. He was not only the porter, but also cleaned all the rooms daily and made sure we had everything we needed or wanted. Somehow the fact that he didn't speak English and we spoke only garbled Sicilian-Italian didn't even matter.

Figure 19. Rosetta, Rosalba and Giacomo Zarba, 1995

La Famiglia

Next we had to telephone the Tolaro and Zarba families but because we were tired—and a bit fearful I must admit—we decided to rest first. So many questions and concerns spun around in my head. *Were the families happy we had made the journey, or would we be imposing ourselves into their lives? How would we talk to each other since we spoke little Italian and, as far as we knew, none of them spoke English?* Just days before our departure from the United States, their letters had arrived, assuring us that my grandmother's younger brother Rocco, three of his children and their families, and two first cousins of my grandfather and their families, would be "waiting to embrace us." That was it. That was all we knew.

We took a little nap to shore up our courage. It was two o'clock.

About three-thirty I startled awake with someone banging on the door. It was my father telling me excitedly that the woman from the desk had telephoned him to say that the family was there downstairs and ... just then my phone began to ring.

The woman's voice was anxious and she spoke too fast. I asked her to speak more slowly, and she did, and after the third or fourth attempt, I realized that she wasn't the woman from the hotel, but in fact, one of our cousins. Dad had hung up on her, having misunderstood her message. (We discovered during our stay that it often required the two of us to get the information correct.)

"This is Masina, the wife of Zarba, Vincenzo" she said, "the son of Zarba, Rocco." Then she told me that the Tolaro and Zarba families would like to come to the hotel at six o'clock to take us to a party.

Dad and I became so excited we could hardly think, but naturally said yes, we would be ready at six. After I hung up the phone we began to ask each other: "What are we going to do in Pietraperzia? What are we going to talk about? How many people will be there? Does anyone speak English?" Then we figured it was out of our hands, and in the hands of the family. To myself, I said, *Che sarà sarà*, as the familiar song goes. *What will be, will be ...*

The three of us decided to take a walk around Caltanissetta and, as we walked, we talked about my grandparents, and thought that they had probably walked on those same streets. I remembered grandma talking about Caltanissetta and finally I was there. It seemed like a dream.

Everything was deserted and quiet then at about four-thirty. They take a long mezzogiorno break we noticed. All the buildings were old, not especially distinctive, made from the same golden-colored blocks, with layers of dirt and car exhaust coating them. The golden hills outside of the town, the wheat fields, the buildings in the town, everything had the look of gold. Old, dirty, burnished gold.

At six we were in the sitting room of the hotel lobby. From there we could see the reception desk and bar through the large double wooden doors that separated the two areas. The room was huge, with plain, utilitarian furniture placed around its perimeter in random conversational groupings—a dark green vinyl sofa, a simple brown wood coffee table, a dark gold chair or two, and a worn brass floor lamp. Even though large windows looked out over the veranda, the thick, heavy forest green coverings kept the late afternoon light from shining in.

Mom and I sat nervously on the sofa nearest the door facing the windows. Dad sat for a few minutes and then paced about, from the lobby to the sitting area, to the porch, and so on. After about ten or fifteen minutes he suddenly came running in, shouting "they're here, they're here ... and there are carloads of them!"

The tranquil hotel lobby quickly filled with noise and activity. Signor Luigi and the others watched, stunned, as our relatives burst into the reception area and on into the sitting room. They grabbed each one of us, hugging and kissing us with tears streaming from their eyes. "Tolaro, Tolaro, Zarba, Tolaro, Zarba, Zarba," each one said as we embraced. It seemed to go on for a long time because so many people of all ages kept entering and racing up, grabbing us and talking on and on in Italian I had certainly never heard before. My head was spinning from the overwhelming display as I looked around in disbelief at the thirty to thirty-five people.

It became calm then, the conversations subdued, arms tightly embracing one another. Everyone stared toward the double doors as Zio Rocco shuffled slowly into the room on the arm of his son Vincenzo: Maria Calogera's younger brother, eighty-five years old, the only one of the six siblings still alive. When I saw him my heart filled with so much joy, like it would have if my grandmother had suddenly been standing there. He was a small man, short and delicate, whose face reminded me of hers. I could see that he was proud and loving by the set of his jaw and his eyes, blue and lively like his sister's.

I will never forget the moment when, with tears in our eyes we embraced, and he repeated over and over again, with quiet happiness, so close to my ear that I could feel the warmth of his breath, "Ora, sono contento ... sono contento," telling me, without my having had to ask him, that he was content to have finally met the American family of his lovely sister.

And so, with great joy, my Sicilian family truly embraced my American family, and announced to the three of us "Andiamo . . . a casa" and we all went ... home.

I had no way of knowing then, of course, that my heart's journey home had just begun.

Figure 20. Wedding of Masina and Vincenzo, c. 1940

Figure 21. Cousins Giovanni, Philip and Giuseppe Tolaro with Totò

Figure 22. Sicilian and American Families – Welcoming Party, June 1989

Figure 23. Family outing to the Castle, 1989

Home

None of us would ever forget that evening. Confusion dominated, with us Americans always the center of attention and with so many cousins' names to remember. Zio Rocco never left my father's side, whose own expression was indescribable. I understood that I had not only realized my dream, but also given joy to others. The families had found a local young woman Borina, who had grown up in Boston, and she became our translator. We were shocked when she introduced herself at the Albergo Di Prima because she had, of course, a very strong Boston accent. Our Sicilian family welcomed us in a truly exceptional manner. Home always feels warm and physical. That evening I felt at home.

How can this be, we think,

Wandering, dreamlike, among the people.

This is coming home in some miraculous, magical

Inexplicable way. We've really only been here before

With them and the lives we suppose they lived, in

Stories over the years. Rich images contradict the old,

Used-up empty grayness,

filled often with poverty and sadness.

Somehow Maria Calogera managed to color

The gray with the love and strength

she herself lived from day to day.

And now we are here to move among her people, our people,

At once strangers and family.

Figure 24. Family of Zio Rocco: Masina, Vincenzo, Zio Rocco, Maria, Lillo, Damiana, Filippo, Graziella, Rosario

Figure 25. Enthusiastic members of Gruppo Folklorico Siciliano

Wildflowers in the Castle Wall

These impressions are from our first visit in 1989. The town officials opened the Castle gate and accompanied us the day we visited the site. Most of the local family had never entered either and it was an exciting excursion for young and old alike, even my cousins in their proper high heel pumps! In fact, it was quite dangerous considering its run-down condition. Now the area has been turned into a local destination, the Belvedere, because of the expansive view of the sweeping countryside, which on certain clear days even includes Mount Etna.

The ruins of the giant castle rise above Pietraperzia, a town whose ancient roots reach back to the Neolithic age, about 3,500 B.C. The limestone caves, where the first inhabitants lived, stand in clumps looking like neighborhoods of pierced rocks (pietra = rock, perzia = pierced, according to one theory). The Sicani and Siculi, the two aboriginal peoples of Sicily, inhabited them at different times.

The remains of the medieval bastion stand in the area of some of those original cave enclaves, called *contrade*. The Arabs began the actual edifice as a fortress in the late ninth century A.D. Subsequently, the French Normans (1100s) and the German Swabians (1200s) added to its dimensions and design.

The remaining giant walls look down over the people today just as it has for centuries, since before the Barresi family was granted their barony under feudal Swabian rule. It is and has been crumbling piece by piece. Mounds of yellow and gray rocks lay everywhere and giant gaps in the floor reveal secret tunnels, which connected room after room in the mega-roomed colossus. Town legend says that eventually there were over four hundred fifty rooms, and that once two women went in, got lost, and never came out.

Each wing is constructed differently, depending on the conqueror and the era, mirroring the history of Sicily itself, with the constant foreign invasions that changed the flow and design of her past.

Today though, the castle is ruined. Dead some people might say, with only a few walls still standing, thrusting up into the sky, a monument to its past.

"Just like the town itself is an empty tomb," some of my American family would admonish. That is what I expected. "No one lives there now," others warned me, with deprecation in their voices. "It's dead, nothing's left of the town and the people. Don't bother. Go for an afternoon, or a day, perhaps, but for heaven's sake, don't stay there."

True, after all, grandma and grandpa are both dead, and probably anyone who knew them too. If the rumors were correct, no one would want to live there anymore. Gray darkness. That is what I had always imagined: a bleak town in the uncompromising Sicilian sun. Then, I would imagine again the warm, loving arms of my grandmother around me, and continue to dream of the day I would find out.

I had never heard about the castle before, or maybe my image of Pietraperzia might have been filled with more majesty and hope for the family's ancestral home. My grandmother had never ever mentioned it in her stories. To her though it was no doubt just a pile of rocks that had no meaning in the day-to-day struggle they faced to survive in the early twentieth century.

Now I know about it though.

Just as wildflowers of every color—red, yellow, purple, orange, blue—grow out of the cracks and crevices of the castle walls, and cover the floors that nature has reclaimed, handsome children and cousins, grow in the town I had believed dead. Their cheeks are bright and their voices happy and lively as they play in the ancient streets at the foot of the castle, where my grandparents and generations before them walked. They go to school and sing their songs, the old ones that my grandma sang and taught me, and the new ones that my own children sing. They still manage to cherish the old ones, while reaching for the new.

Pietraperzia is alive. Life is better for some than for others. It is never easy. However, just as those flowers grow out of the castle's ruins, life continues for the people out of the cracks and crevices of the old world in which they were born. Look at the children. Their faces do not lie. Pietraperzia is alive.

PIETRAPERZIA - Il Castello

Figure 26. The Castle, Pietraperzia, 1900

Figure 27. Santa Maria Maggiore, 'La Matrice' – the Mother Church, c. 1900

Figure 28. Via Barone Tortorici toward La Matrice

Custodian of the Family Soul

My grandmother often talked about the church where she and my grandfather had been married and managing to enter inside the structure that was at that time in need of repair was a very important moment for all of us. Again, most of the Sicilian family had not been able to enter for generations. Now it has been beautifully restored and many of the town's most important celebrations take place inside.

That shining mid-June day, with a cloudless sky and red geraniums spilling off every balcony overlooking the piazza, I found myself dizzy in the midst of Sicilian Tolaros and Zarbas. We stood at the foot of the wide, flat, rough-chiseled stone stairs leading up to shabby former Santa Maria di Gesù, later Santa Maria Maggiore. Its rickety wooden outer doors with green paint peeling, hung askew in dilapidated weariness. Now revered as La Matrice, the Mother Church, the unspectacular, unfinished matriarch lacked even a trace of the beauty I had always imagined as my grandmother had described her wedding day. Constructed of the same tired golden-tan blocks that characterized all the buildings in the town, it resembled a warehouse, big, plain, and utilitarian. Its flat front lacked even a portico, and with the exception of the three front doors, a small ledge located a few feet from the top and a high central panel that reached upward, ending in a point and a crucifix, nothing relieved the rectangular plainness. *Strange*, I thought silently, *a strange beauty that I do not understand.* I felt a foreigner and sad. *Sometimes it is better to live with romantic images than to face reality* ... weighed heavily inside me.

We cousins waited anxiously outside while one of the many named Salvatore went to find the custodian and procure the key. La Matrice was closed indefinitely, in dangerous disrepair. The 25 or so family members were flitting between the small, animated groups we had formed, everyone talking at once, as usual. Excited to show us *cugini americani* the precious jewel of their town, they felt privileged to enter its sacred doors. Disappointed and tired then, I struggled to communicate in my poor Italian. Borina, our translator could not join us that day. Salvatore finally returned and, opening the old central door, we filed in.

Filtered cool light, like heaven had unlocked itself to us, welcomed expectant eyes, bathing and refreshing the whole body. All at once, a hush enveloped the spirited group, huddled together at the back facing the altar that seemed to float in shimmering air. We wrapped arms tightly around each other, a mass of Sicilians and Americans together, tears streaming down our cheeks. Even ten year old Vincenzo, who usually darted here and there, full of energy and minimally involved in the evolving reunion, bashfully sidled close to my father, his face an uncanny echo of my dad's own childhood photo framed on the piano at my home in California.

Tearfully my parents and I recreated the wedding day, realizing that for the first time we stood where Maria Calogera and Filippo had stood on October 27, 1913. We had already walked the ancient streets of the town and imagined their footsteps of the past. However, inside La Matrice we knew with certainty that our footprints matched the old ones.

Their sure presence surrounded us, the soft celestial light soaking into our pores. Maria Calogera and Filippo's rite of initiation bonded us to Pietraperzia and the people, as if my grandparents had been waiting patiently for our arrival. Like their marriage had joined them together so many years ago, inside the chiesa at that moment, the Sicilian and American Tolaros and Zarbas together promised solemnly to hold dear the past that we share and approach the present and future together.

Later we meandered slowly throughout the church, looking closely at details pointed out, mostly by the women in the group. We understood grandma's lifelong attachment to the Sacred Heart and Saint Vincent when we saw the two doll-like, much revered, painted plaster statues honored there. The interior seemed gaudy on close inspection. Little genuine marble and precious gold decorated it. Inexpensive, nonfunctioning chandeliers dangled precariously. Old candles leaned in tarnished holders on the altar painted to look like green, pink and white marble. Small, threadbare Persian carpets lay here and there in front of the altar. Way in the back, in a dark forgotten corner, stood the sarcophagus of the Principessa Dorotea, beloved patron of the town and the church during the fifteenth century.

That June day, however, we hardly noticed its brokenness. We felt instead the strong soul of La Matrice and the spirit of communion with our Sicilian family. I decided as we closed the door behind us that . . . *no, reality is better than a dream unfulfilled.*

Love Story

This is a granddaughter's imagined vision of her grandparents' love story based on both her grandmother and Zio Rocco's narrations. Two truths emerge: Maria Calogera was a very courageous, independent-minded woman for the times and my grandparents' love for each other over the years vindicates her decision to follow her heart. As their granddaughter I experienced first hand their loving, devoted relationship—her Prince Charming and his Queen Maria Calogera, as he always referred to her.

Pietraperzia, Sicily – November 1913

Maria Calogera took a deep breath, stood as tall as her four-foot, 10-inch frame would allow, stuck out her chin bravely, and knocked on her parents' door. The door flew open. Her father Vincenzo had been waiting for her, ready to explode into tears or anger, perhaps both. Their blue eyes locked: father Vincenzo's in authority, daughter Maria Calogera's in audacity. Damiana, her mother, was in the shadows at the back of the large family's dwelling. She was sobbing, as she had been for days. Not much was private in the close confines and stark reality of Pietraperzia, or of the Zarba family. The

town was small and poor, in central Sicily. The Zarba family was poor, landless.

Giuseppina, Maria Calogera's eleven-year-old sister, hovered next to their mother. Francesca, a sickly younger sister, lay on the bed. Brothers Giovanni, nine-year-old Rocco, and Salvatore were perhaps out scrabbling for work in the streets and fields. Only the father and his oldest child, the one standing at the door, spoke. She had married Filippo

Figure 29. Filippo Tolaro & Maria Calogera Zarba, Winter, c. 1940

51

Tolaro on October 27 and moved to a house nearby, bought by the twenty-two-year-old with money he had earned in America. He was a good match for her, and for the family: a landowner already. However, a few days earlier the nineteen-year-old woman had announced that she and her new husband would soon leave for the United States. She was returning that November afternoon to give her parents further details and, she hoped, to get their blessing.

Pietraperzia- Corso Vittorio Emanuele

Figure 30. Piazza Santa Maria, Pietraperzia, Sicily, c. 1900

Maria Calogera's beauty stood out in a culture defined by dark. The daughter's hair, the color of shining copper, was pulled back into a braided bun. The people in the paese referred to her as "la ragazza con il viso splendente come la luna," the young woman with the face as beautiful as the moon, because her luminescent skin, the color of ivory, shone so differently than the normally dark-complexioned townspeople. It would be possible to drown in the spell cast by the older sister's striking blue eyes, which looked out over high cheekbones. Even at nineteen, she had a regal air, in spite of the family circumstances. She was one of the town's most handsome young women, a prize for her family to barter, a prize for the one who would win her heart. With the recent arrival of Filippo, her nameless prince had arrived, the one who would take her away. She was ready to leave with him; her parents were not prepared to lose her.

"No, please don't go. You don't have to go with him. Stay here with your family, as you should," her father urged.

The young woman, already prepared for the scene she would face, tried to comfort him by saying "Filippo has money and a job with the railroad waiting for him in New Hampshire. I will have a good life. He is a fine man. You don't have to worry about me. I want to go. I want to be with him. You have arranged a good match for me."

Figure 31. Three Vincenzo Zarbas with San Vincenzo, La Matrice, 1989.
Great-nephew and two nephews of Maria Calogera Zarba, sons of
brothers Salvatore and Rocco.

"No," he continued, "no, I forbid it. You will stay here. Filippo lied to us, Maria Calogera," Vincenzo insisted. "We thought you would stay in Pietraperzia because he bought a house in the paese. He bought land to cultivate in the countryside and a mule to work it. We allowed you to marry him only after we believed you would stay here with your family. He tricked us. The priest has told us that the church will annul the marriage. You must let him go."

Figure 32. Downtown Bellows Falls, 1909

And Maria Calogera responded, "I'm sorry, Papà, but Filippo is my husband now, and I will go where he goes." With that, she turned away and left her home forever.

The Legacy: North Walpole – 1950s

I grew up listening to the love story of Maria Calogera Zarba and Filippo Tolaro, and the accompanying saga of trickery and anger, from her, my grandmother. "One evening," she would recount "while parading with the other young bachelors on their *passeggiata* (walk) before supper, your grandfather Filippo saw me combing my long hair on the balcony overlooking the street. The young women were not permitted to walk unaccompanied, so we would perch above, on our balconies, primping and flirting, looking over the crop of eligible bachelors strutting below. I had heard the gossip of his surprise return to Pietraperzia, but I didn't know who he was. He had left Pietraperzia when he was fourteen and I had been too young to notice him. We all expected that he had returned to find a wife to take to America, and I understood that evening on my balcony, when our eyes met, that he liked me. And I liked him too." That's how the story began.

My grandfather always made it clear that Maria Calogera's beauty captured his heart at first sight. Whenever he described her on the balcony, combing her auburn hair as it hung in waves to her waist, I could feel my gruff but gentle grandpa's mind slip back to that evening in his hometown, when he saw his queen, as he always called her, the love of his life.

He had indeed returned to the town to find a wife to bring back to New Hampshire, where he had a job and the possibility to build a good life. In going through the family documents before the beginning of my own journey back to Pietraperzia, I discovered that he had already booked the return ship passage to New York for him and a 'wife'. After seeing my grandmother on the balcony that evening, he had asked his godmother to approach my great-grandfather Vincenzo Zarba to arrange the marriage. He declined the offer believing that Filippo would take her away to America, so Filippo bought the house in the town, the land in the countryside, and the mule to work it. We were able to visit the house and the land, which after their departure belonged to members of the Zarba family. He had indeed tricked the Zarba family into believing that he would remain in the town after the marriage. However, my grandmother Maria Calogera made the courageous choice to follow her young husband Filippo to America, where my story began.

In 1989 I asked her brother Zio Rocco to relate the details of the story of my grandparents' marriage and departure from Pietraperzia in November 1913, anxious to compare versions. He did so and seemed to enjoy the part that confirmed my grandfather's ability to find a wife; obtain permission to marry her (after buying a house, land, and a mule); file for a passport for said new wife; marry her; and take her away—all in twenty-two days!

Figure 33. 40th Anniversary with seven of their eight children, 1953

I grew up in a village, Bellows Falls, Vermont, across the Connecticut River from North Walpole, New Hampshire, where they lived. I was accustomed to seeing my grandparents Filippo and Maria Calogera, walking hand in hand: in the town Square, along the river, or on our summer evening outings, up the dirt road of the hill behind their house. For me they were always royalty, the king and his prized queen. We would sit on their screened-in front porch on summer evenings, watching the world go by. They would tell me stories, captivating stories, about Sicily and Pietraperzia, and the people from the past.

Grandpa died in 1959 when I was twelve, and grandma always carried his memory and her love for him in her heart until her own death in 1980. They never went back to Pietraperzia. But I did, on their behalf, and I brought their son, my father Philip, and Rita my mother with me, along with another generation of Tolaro-Zarba progeny. And the family's story continues because of a love story so long ago ...

Figure 34. Mary took this last photo of her grandparents together, 1959

Figure 35. 40th Anniversary with grandchildren, 1953. Grandchildren, from left to right, Philip, Larry, Mary and Terry.

Figure 36. Giovanni with his father, Cesare, receiving the
Onoreficienza di Cavaliere

But Poor Zio Giovanni

Family! This was my first lesson in trying to understand a culture so different from my own. Often my later stories also reflect this confusion and the moments of enlightenment when misadventures become adventures and the journey empowering.

Mom, dad and I were eating a relaxed breakfast on Thursday morning, the day after we had arrived, luxuriating in the afterglow of the previous evening's events, when Signor Luigi came to get us for a phone call. After the call, we had a dilemma on our hands. Zio Giovanni Tolaro insisted that we sleep at their house that night, but we had already declined an invitation offered by the Zarbas. We already had our rooms reserved at the hotel and thought we should keep our plans intact, especially since Tom and our two sons would be arriving on Sunday. Dad felt we should accept Zio Giovanni's invitation though—I believe he did not know how to say no without causing hurt feelings. To keep peace, we offered to spend one night at the home of a Zarba cousin too. Arrangements were made for him to pick us up at the hotel at five o'clock.

He and his son Totò arrived right on time, so we gathered our smallish bags and reluctantly said goodbye to our friends at the hotel, telling them we would not return until Saturday evening. Then Zio Giovanni informed me that I had to drive our van to Pietraperzia, which had not been in the original plan proposed that morning.

Zio Giovanni was a short man with facial features that reminded me of the Tolaros I had grown up with, maybe 5'6" and probably in his early sixties. He used his hands excitedly as he gave us orders, like a man who was used to having them met without a fuss. Totò stood quietly shifting from one foot to the other, black eyes nervously bouncing back and forth in a matching rhythm. Short, slight, with very dark hair, thick bushy black eyebrows and a mustache to match, he was in his early thirties.

Since I was not anxious to move the van out of the parking space I had miraculously fit into the day before, dad and I questioned our uncle gently. We tried to make sense out of why I had to drive when he had his car there and we could have all fit in easily, but to no avail.

Zio wanted me to drive to Pietraperzia for some undefined reason, and that was that. He would ride with me as navigator, and mom and dad would ride with Totò in the Alfa Romeo.

So I said fine then, let's go, and my parents looked at me with fear in their eyes as they went off. I was more miffed than nervous now because it seemed like Zio Giovanni was trying to run things and change plans that everyone else had set. *Oh well*, I thought to myself, *it can't be as bad as the drive through Palermo!*

Figure 37. Zio Giovanni's family with Mom, Dad and Mary, June 1992

As we walked down the steep driveway to get to the garage I explained to him clearly, I thought, that all he had to do was tell me *a destra* or *a sinistra* when we came to an intersection. I knew he didn't know any English, so I wanted to assure him that he could use Italian to give me directions and I would understand, maybe, I hoped.

At any rate I was trying to be positive about the turn of events. I was not pleased about giving up the calm of my hotel room at night, to be perfectly honest, and at that moment, Zio Giovanni was not on my favorite relative list.

He didn't respond really, he just walked looking straight ahead as if I was not even there. Okay, I thought, I surely hope he knows the way, because I don't. After unlocking the gate so I could get the van,

60

Salvatore, the porter, followed us, intending to direct me out of the garage and the minuscule lot. He would be lucky if I didn't accidentally run over him in that postage stamp space.

We got to the van, I deactivated the alarm, and Zio Giovanni and I opened the doors and climbed in. It was a giant step up for him too. His dark, intense, almost black eyes said that he had obviously not expected to ride in a truck. I should have picked up that clue, but instead I began to pay more attention to the task at hand than to him.

I put the key in the ignition, turned it sharply to the right as I gave it a little gas, and we promptly lurched forward into the stonewall because I had forgotten to put down the clutch. I successfully started it the second time, got it into reverse and we were on our way. I breathed a big sigh of relief. I knew the worst was over. Remember I was trying to be positive. I was even a little proud of myself I suppose. The porter Salvatore directed as I jockeyed the big van back and forth and to this side and that turning around so we could head out and up the driveway front first. Backing up would have been impossible for me because of its steep, narrowness. Hey, I handled it well. No problem.

I turned left onto Via Kennedy at the top of the driveway, and hoped for the best. Zio Giovanni still had not said a word. When I came to the first intersection the only direction he gave me was a big—like a large American pizza pie—counterclockwise circular motion with his right arm and a sound resembling a deep internal sigh, which I guessed meant, bear to the left. Whew, I happened to be right! My confidence soared.

Traffic was heavy because everyone was on his or her way back to work after the mezzogiorno break, another rush hour in Caltanissetta, and we were in the thick of it. I really do not remember all the specific lefts and rights we took to get out of the city, but they probably totaled five or six, and my instruction from the navigator each time we approached an intersection consisted of the identical counterclockwise circular motion in the air with his right arm, and the nondescript sigh. Amazingly, I only misunderstood one time, and then poor Zio seemed overly distraught. However, I corrected the mistake easily and we were on our way to Pietraperzia.

I was getting excited. The night before we had only seen the town on its hill from a distance on our way as passengers to the campagna for the party. I looked forward to the first glimpse of its actual ancient streets. That is what I had been waiting for.

The road from Caltanissetta to the smaller town was as crooked as any I had ever been on and very narrow. We climbed steadily for about ten or fifteen minutes, and every few feet made a blind turn in the opposite direction, as the road curved back and forth over and over again.

Figure 38. Pietraperzia with Caltanisetta in the distance

I was actually pretty proud of the way I was driving the White Whale by then, even though my jerky shifting hinted at my inexperience as we climbed the curvy mountain road. *I haven't stalled once since that first time*, I thought.

Then I noticed my poor uncle. He was clutching the seat under him with both hands, knuckles white, and face too, all tense like he expected the next curve to be his last. And I had thought I was doing so well. When I looked at him he uttered, in Sicilian-Italian, the only words he said on the whole trip: "And does your husband also drive?" in dialect of course.

Without thinking I said "yes, and so does our son," the thought of which seemed to frighten him even more. Then, for one reason or another I started to look at the situation from his perspective, and realized the trauma this poor Sicilian gentleman was experiencing.

Zio Giovanni, at least one generation older than I, did not drive (I discovered this later), and was face to face with, not only a generation gap, but also a clash of cultures. As we started out he was probably not sure about riding with a woman driver, since many of the women my age or older in his world did not drive. Then we got into the big van, which was certainly the only one I had seen on our visit. What really set the tone for the trip though was my forgetting the clutch at the beginning, when we lurched so unexpectedly right into the wall. Poor Zio had not given me verbal instructions because he was too scared and could not speak. At that moment I felt badly for not realizing the situation, and trying to make him feel more comfortable. Instead I had been preoccupied with my own fears, which then seemed minor compared to his.

We arrived safely at the mountaintop, and after descending carefully, so as not to scare him more than I already had, we traveled a short distance on a straightaway, which brought us right to Pietraperzia's perimeter. We made a left turn and there we were!

Zio Giovanni directed me in his usual manner to his house; I stopped the van, disembarked, locked it, set the alarm and greeted with surprise all the relatives who had congregated to meet us. My folks had not arrived though.

In about five minutes they pulled up in Totò's car, panicking because they had not seen us along the way. They had followed as we turned out of the driveway in Caltanissetta, and had expected to keep us in sight. They imagined the worst, as parents do, of course, worried that something bad had happened, like we had gone the wrong way or I had been kidnapped.

Luckily, all of our fears were unjustified because everyone had indeed arrived safely. Yes, I could get that darn van out of the tiny spot, and even follow Zio's directions. Yes, he could ride in a truck with a woman driver and not end up in a ditch, or worse. Yes, their daughter Mary could get in a car with a somewhat unfamiliar relative in an unknown place and arrive unharmed, in better spirits than when she had left, and in record time.

Figure 39. Zio Giovanni with grandson Emanuele, 1990

Figure 40. Cousin Daniela Marotta with Gruppo Folklorico Siciliano, 1989

Figure 41. Ausilia & Roberto's wedding, 1995

Figure 42. Maria Calogera and Filippo, c. 1950

On Reaching

Sometimes fear has kept me from reaching out, looking beyond the confines I have often created for myself: fear of failure, fear of creating a disturbance, fear of the unknown, fear of . . . the list could on and on. However, in spite of my trepidation I did reach out to our Sicilian family and learned the value of taking a chance.

I stood there
In the room teaming with activity:
Twenty-five young folk dancers and
Musicians gathered around my sons,
Talking and laughing; Father Bongiovanni
Deep in conversation with Mom and Dad,
Giacomo and Zio Giovanni;
Smiling Zio Rocco with his arm slung over
Granddaughter Paola's shoulder affectionately;
Tom and the two Vincenzos with laughter in their eyes
And hearts, like the other sixty or so people
Outside and inside and everywhere I looked.
I realized suddenly that one letter
In tortured Italian, filled with hope,
Had allowed it to
Happen.

Imagining the Family Embrace

Since I am the lone chronicler these are my observations of what that first visit meant to some of the elderly participants. All have passed away now, more than twenty-five years later, but the memory of my conversations with them and their feelings at the time never fail to bring me a smile as I look back and remember their words.

Philip Tolaro Says:

I never thought I would be in Sicily, the land of my parents, and meet an uncle, aunt and so many cousins I can't count them. That first night was something I'll never forget because what we expected and what happened was so amazing. We expected a handful of people, and we hoped they were getting along–Tolaros and Zarbas–because of the story we'd heard about Pop tricking Mom's family and taking her to New Hampshire in 1913. We were instead met by carloads of them at the hotel, from the very young to the very old, and taken to a huge party in the campagna, Tolaros and Zarbas together. I would guess maybe fifty to sixty people were there. I was so overcome with excitement and intense emotion that I couldn't even think, but somehow, I was able to talk to all of these wonderful people from the dialect I had heard when I was growing up. I missed my brothers and sisters at that time. It would have been perfect if we all could have been together there, with so many of our relatives. Lord willing, that day will come. We ate and drank, and saluted each other and Mom and Pop, and sang and hung onto each other in disbelief. It was a dream, but one that has continued since, and my life would never be the same.

Rita Tolaro Says:

Well, I loved Mom and Pop and I love Phil and my joy was seeing him fulfill a dream he has always had, sort of like retiring to Florida was too. I don't know any Italian, so I couldn't talk to many of the people, but somehow we managed to communicate. They showed as much love for me as for Phil. I tried to fit in and everyone got such a big kick out of me because I learned one new Italian word a day—*basta* was the first, at mealtime. I couldn't begin to eat what they would put on my plate. *Buon giorno* was a little tricky, but they all clapped and carried on whenever I tried. It tickled me to see Phil with his relatives at last. When we went in the church where Mom and Pop were married we all broke down. We could just picture them there on their wedding day. I think that was one of the really special moments, to say a prayer in their church. Mom always loved Santa Maria. We laughed a lot that week, everyone was so happy. I was thrilled when my son-in-law Tom, and grandsons Jim and Phil joined Mary, Phil and me on Sunday though. Finally I had my boys there and we could speak English! Four generations were together—Zio Rocco, Phil, Mary, and Jim and Philip. It was like a dream. I wished Mom and Pop could have been there too.

Figure 43. Wedding of Philip Tolaro and Rita Thibodeaux, April 22, 1946

Speaking for the Relatives:

All in all we think it went well. At first we didn't know what to expect. After all it had been so long since we'd had any news. They seemed to come because they really wanted to know us, although we had some uneasiness before we met them. Perhaps they wanted to claim the land and the house that Filippo had bought before he took Maria Calogera away. Of course those thoughts go through your mind when out of the blue something like this happens. And why hadn't they kept in touch? They wanted to see so much and had so many questions. They fit in. They really were family. It was a hectic time, and full of joy. We couldn't show them everything; the time was too short. Maybe on another visit they will stay longer so we can get to know each other better. We have so much time to make up. They brought us many pictures and much news about our American family. Some of us had never believed that our relatives really do live in the Stati Uniti because we had never heard from them. They brought us gifts, little things to remind us of them and America, and an album for each family with pictures of Filippo and Maria Calogera, their children, grandchildren and great-grandchildren. It was over before we knew it. Saying goodbye was difficult, not knowing when and if we would see each other again. It was like a dream, a beautiful dream that the photographs and letters prove really did happen.

Figure 44. Dad sharing our gift photo album, 1989

Figure 45. Nina Tolaro's wedding with Aunt, Uncle, and Cousins

Zio Giuseppe Tolaro Says:

This visit of my American cousins pleased my family and me very much. Filippo Tolaro and my brothers and I were young together, and meeting his son and family reminds me of those days again, of life in Pietraperzia as a child. We lived very close to each other and I showed them on Friday, that I lived upstairs with my family and he lived downstairs right next door. He left in 1905 for America the first time when he was only fourteen years old. I was younger than him, and always thought how brave he was to take off like that. He came back once and married Maria Calogera Zarba from our town and left almost immediately for America again. That was the last we ever saw or heard from him or his family. Most of the younger people in the family did not believe us when we told them that we had American cousins. Well, they have seen for themselves.

It was like a dream that after seventy-six years I once again meet a Filippo Tolaro, his son, who had so much interest in everything about his father. I was happy to know that my cousin loved us enough, and Sicilia too, to make his son want to travel so far to find us again. My cousin seemed real to me again, and no longer just a distant blurry memory fading into the past. The emptiness has been filled with contentment and the circle of the family was once again whole.

Figure 46. Giuseppe Tolaro with Mom and Dad where Filippo had lived

Figure 47. Zio Rocco Zarba, younger brother of Maria Calogera

Zio Rocco Zarba Says:

My oldest sister Maria Calogera left my family and me when I was nine years old, and I remember feeling like my mother had gone because Maria had always taken care of me. I missed her for a long time, but after many years I gave up hoping that I would ever see her again. I used to wonder if in her mind we no longer existed, if she had just forgotten us. I wished she could have met my wife Paola, for them to be friends. But it was not to be, and what can you do? You have to accept these things in life.

When Father Bongiovanni gave us the letter that her granddaughter had written, I couldn't believe it, that at last we would spend time with Maria Calogera's family. So much time had passed since we'd had any news.

The day my nephew Philip, his wife Rita and their daughter Mary arrived, we were all busy preparing for the party at Rosario's house in the campagna—Zarbas and Tolaros together. Philip had made it clear that he would like all of us to be together. When we thought they might be at the hotel my daughter-in-law Masina called and eventually they understood we would meet them there at six o'clock.

Many of us Zarbas and Tolaros went to Caltanissetta to the Albergo Di Prima and there they were! My nephew Philip was on the veranda watching for us and when I saw him I knew my lovely sister had finally come home to us through him and his family. Inside I met his wife and daughter, and we embraced with great joy in our hearts. I rejoiced knowing that at last my American family would again be a part of my life and my family, which means everything to me. I now understand that my sister Maria Calogera and her husband Filippo taught their children to love their family and their heritage. Otherwise, why would they have come to find us?

When we arrived at the festa in their honor, with tears in my eyes I asked my sister's granddaughter if she had brought a picture of Maria Calogera to show me. With my own eyes I wanted to see what she had become, to have an image of her as she really was, rather than the young brother's memory of the girl who had left here in 1913. It was then she and Philip and Rita presented the Zarba family and me with an entire album of photographs, showing Maria Calogera and

Filippo's life in America. I was overcome with emotion as I looked at one page after another of my American family, and I gently kissed each of my dear sister's pictures as I moved slowly from one to the next.

At last I felt connected to her again. "Ora sono contento, sono contento—now I am happy, I am happy."

Figure 48. Mary with Zio Rocco, 1990

Figure 49. Dinner in the countryside with Vincenzo Zarba's family

Fig. 50. Philip Noyes' "Tomato Cluster" inspired by his grandfather, 2016

The Journey Continues

What brings me the most satisfaction during this heart's journey, which officially began in 1989, is the realization that the first visit was more than just a cursory acknowledgement of my American family's connection to Sicily and to the family there. Over the years a bond has been created between us that will hopefully continue, depending on the resolve of future generations. I have returned many times over the years, sometimes alone and other times in the company of other family members, namely my husband Tom, our son Phil, and our niece Melissa. The next two stories highlight the process of building memories that helped to cement our relationship. My stories almost always illustrate that no matter how often I return to visit my Sicilian family the possibility of an adventure and another story will always tempt me.

In August of 1990, my husband Tom and I and our 16-year-old son Phil traveled to Pietraperzia for the second time to visit our newly discovered family.

The Train to Etna documents our first train experience in Italy of the 1990s. Train travel now can be quite different because of the high speed and dedicated tracks; the ticket machines in most stations; the ability to use English; and not to mention booking online. We had a lot to learn on that trip, which began with us believing we were well prepared for our return adventure in Sicily. We had had to save money, so we had no rental car, and only second class 'no reservation' train tickets. We did learn to laugh at our naive selves, grateful for the fun we have had along the way.

Perhaps the trip would be different now, easier, and less fraught with uncertainty. Then too, we would miss the retelling of our tales.

The bustling small town is in the middle of the island between Enna and Caltanissetta and quite remote, especially before the completion of the highway that now links it to the coasts. Its connecting roads were narrow and curvy and went from paved to unpaved regularly and unexpectedly, the ancient stone bridges sometimes spanning a trickling stream or dry river bed that became a gushing torrent after a heavy rain. One was just as likely to meet a shepherd and a herd of lively goats or lazy sheep as another passenger car. With our lack of Italian and overwhelmingly enthusiastic Pietrini cousins as guides, we enjoyed a number of adventures over the years, including the adventure in *Thomas and the Capricious Goats.*

The remaining stories capture a few of the special moments we have experienced. They will probably not be the last ...

Figure 51. Zio Rocco with granddaughter, Paola, 1989

Figure 52. Vincenzo Zarba and Claudio Valverdi with gift headbands, 1989

Figure 53. Mount Etna in the distance at Easter time

The Train to Etna

On the seventh of August 1990 my husband Tom, our sixteen-year-old son Phil, and I got up at 3:30 in the morning to travel from Sorrento to Napoli on the local Cicumvesuvio train. There we were to wait for our train, the 'Treno dell'Etna' that would take us to Catania, Sicily.

Napoli Centrale, On the Train – 7 August 1990

"Good morning," they said to us politely. "Good morning," we responded. It was an awkward moment.

I had waited at the end of one of the Treno dell'Etna's coaches with the six too-heavy bags while the two men went off to find suitable seats. Each train car was made up of a number of compartments, with a door to the corridor that ran the length of the car. The train was very long and crowded, with groups of travelers like us carrying too many bags. Finally Phil returned and explained the plan. They had found some seats in a wagon behind us. I was to go there to hold the seats and Phil would remain with the bags. Then Tom would carry the bags from one car to the other.

When I got to that car, the compartment with six seats seemed full with the four people inside. We would not all be able to fit. There was a family of three or four persons: husband, wife, and an elderly woman of at least 70. There was also a young woman of about twenty years old, who might have been their daughter.

They all looked at us, surprised to see American tourists, and we looked at them timidly, and at their large towels spread over all the seats, including the extra ones. Obviously, they did not want to share their cozy compartment with anyone else. However, in the end they adjusted their bags to make room for ours and reorganized themselves to leave room for Phil and me. I got settled and started updating my journal and Phil listened to music on his Walkman. Tom set out to find another seat, hopefully, close by. It was about 10:00 by then.

Beforehand, we had studied the Orario Generale, the official train schedule and we seemed to have understood it. I had called my cousin Giacomo in Pietraperzia to give him the particulars of our journey and arrival time (HA!). He and Vincenzo would meet us at Catania Centrale and bring us to Pietraperzia in their car. We had brought some bread and cheese, mineral water, and fruit for meals. Phil had lots of spare batteries for his Walkman and we had books to pass the time during the nine to ten hour train ride. We felt prepared and ready to go.

Figure 54. Zia Paola and Zio Rocco and family, c. 1950s

In fact, we had a lot to learn about the train system and ourselves as the day progressed. For instance, that "Express" train number 899 would be 30 minutes late (actually not bad, considering later experiences) and meet us at a different track than was posted. Tom had left us at binario eight and gone for a quick check at the central information point and when our train did arrive, Phil had to take four of the six heavy bags, none with wheels in those early days, from one track to the other while I looked for my husband. Fortunately, he was close by casually studying how train cars were linked to each other. In the meantime, Phil brought all the bags to track twelve and we all managed to get on the train at the last minute. We had no idea where we were on the train, or if there were any seats, but we were at least all on the correct train and our bags were too. One battle won!

Figure 55. Boston & Maine Railroad, Bellows Falls, c. 1920

The Americans Meet the Sicilians

Meanwhile, I overheard the conversation of the other passengers. Elena was lively, probably in her mid-forties. Her light brown hair was short and very curly. Her round face was animated and her blue eyes friendly. Usually it was her voice that dominated the conversation. She was dressed in brown pants and a white knit blouse with the English words 'American Style' written elegantly in black script across the front. At a certain point I sensed she wanted to speak with us.

The elderly signora, Damiana, was Elena's mother. She seemed distant with everyone and spoke only with her daughter. Dressed all in black, her eyes were dark and sorrowful. Damiana never looked at any of the others, just Elena.

Giovanni, Elena's husband was quiet. Short, like the others, he was bald, and smoked constantly in the corridor, thank goodness. He wore dark trousers and a red, gray, and white checked sport shirt. It was not clear if he stayed in the corridor only to smoke, or to get away from the crowded compartment, or perhaps because his wife's constant chatter bothered him. He never said a word.

At first I thought that the young woman Laura was the daughter of Elena and Giovanni, but later understood that she too was a stranger, although Sicilian as they were. The family had already absorbed her into their circle. She was twenty-two years old and wore blue jeans and a pink top. The waves of her long black curly hair framed her pretty face. She slept a lot, read a little, and smoked with Giovanni outside the compartment in the corridor. She hardly spoke. She seemed nice and a little shy.

Toward Sicily

At about 11:30 I left the compartment and went into the corridor to look at the countryside as the train chugged along. I could hear Tom talking English to someone in another compartment and Phil was sleeping. From Napoli we were crossing the regions of Campania and had made stops at Salerno, Battipaglia and Torre Orsaia. Fields of brown earth were full of green plants laden with bright red, ready-to-harvest tomatoes.

As I stood there and watched the world pass by the window, the terrain began to change. Suddenly I felt like I was back in Ohio, with tall hardwood trees punctuating rolling green hills. *This is the reason to travel by train,* I thought. *Italy is beautiful, as all the photos promise, and the people on the train? I don't yet know what to expect. We'll see . . .*

It was an extremely hot day and the inside of the train compartment felt like a too hot oven. The sun beat down relentlessly and there were no protective clouds or even the whisper of a cooler breeze. With the train window open in the corridor, the hot air and dirt from the train tracks sprayed me in the face, and still managed to offer a modicum of relief.

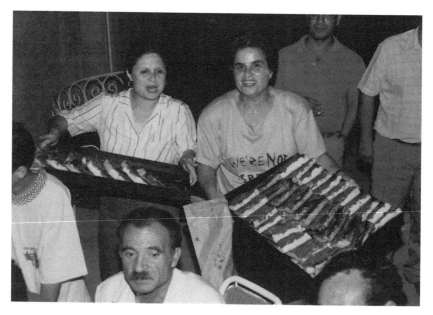

Figure 56. Pizza for dinner in *campagna* (countryside)

Pranzo – Lunch

When I returned to the compartment an hour later, Elena, Giovanni, and Damiana had just begun to eat their pranzo. *Wow,* I thought, *they really know how to eat well and elegantly on a train in a crowded second-class compartment!* Each one had placed a small, richly embroidered cloth on his or her lap and they were all eating small sandwiches filled with prosciutto crudo and mortadella. On the side were containers of green and black olives, red peppers, tiny onions, and artichokes, all dressed in olive oil and vinegar. Then there was a mixed green salad, along with chunks of fresh bread, red wine, orange soda, and mineral water.

The family generously offered a little something to Laura and to us too. Laura accepted a piece of bread and a few of the appetizers. I remembered my Sicilian grandmother, Maria Calogera, admonishing us as children to always politely refuse when offered food—at least two times! I respectfully refused in my very basic Italian and thanked them for their generosity, trying to explain that we had brought our own food and I was waiting for my husband before we too would eat.

Tom arrived shortly thereafter and Phil and Laura decided to go into the corridor to make room for him. Upon his arrival though, Elena evidently decided to try again to break through our shyness. She came up very close to me, actually right in my face, and insisted, "here, signora, you must try this cheese. It's exquisite!"

In fact, I could not say no. She was so close to my face with a short knife and a chunk of wonderfully aromatic cheese right under my nose that I accepted with a reticent smile and "grazie." I was having difficulty understanding her heavily accented Italian. It would compare to an Italian after a few English lessons trying to have an extended conversation with a Texan. I fervently hoped I would not have to converse during the rest of our voyage. We still had hours to face together in the little compartment.

"The cheese is very good," I answered as best I could. "Where are you going?" I continued.

At that point Giovanni and Damiana joined the conversation and explained that they were going to Catania where they live. They had been visiting family in Torino for two weeks and were on their way home.

Then Elena quickly asked where we were going. She added, "Taormina?"

Without thinking too much, I answered that we were not normal American tourists and our destination was not Taormina.

"But why, signora?" she asked. "I don't understand."

With my rudimentary Italian I explained that we were going to Pietraperzia, a little town in the center of Sicily between Enna and

Caltanissetta.

All at once a party erupted in the compartment. Everyone started talking at once and passed us glasses of wine.

"Alla salute!" we all exclaimed together. "To your health!" And "Alla famiglia!

With much difficulty, I explained how a year ago I had found our Sicilian family and, joined by my father and mother, we had visited the family for the first time in almost eighty years because we wanted to know them better and reconnect. They all listened with tears in their eyes and shaking their heads in disbelief as they smiled. "The family lost had become the family recovered!"

At the same time, they continued to pass the food: peaches, melon, caffè, an assortment of cookies and chocolates. *Madonna mia*, I thought, *it seems we have another Sicilian family!*

In the meantime, Phil and Laura returned and the party continued. Our new friends excitedly explained our story to Laura, who happened to be from Caltanisstta herself. Then Elena went directly to Phil and put her left arm on his shoulder, and with the right hand affectionately grabbed his chin, looking in his startled eyes like a long-lost aunt.

Figure 57. Harvesting almonds, Pietraperzia, c. 1920

Late Arrival

Often it seemed the train had been at a standstill more than it had been moving. Then we understood that an 'Espresso' train is just a little better than a local one. We were often stopped because it had to allow the faster trains to speed past. Some of those waiting periods were quite long and eventually we realized that our arrival in Catania would be hours late. We were not even close to Villa San Giovanni in Calabria, at the toe of Italy, where our train would be disengaged and each car brought on to the immense ferry to cross the Strait of Messina. At the arrival there, the train would have to be reassembled. From Messina we would still have a distance to travel further south to Catania.

We began to worry about our cousins who were supposed to meet us at Catania Centrale. In 1990 no one had a cell phone we could use to call and warn them. We hoped they would not just leave the station and go back to Pietraperzia in frustration, thinking we had made a mistake. Our new friends understood that we were worried and I tried to explain the problem. Elena took control immediately.

"Don't worry, signora," she assured me with a smile and an affectionate embrace. "You are not alone now. We will not leave you at the station by yourselves, but take you home with us to spend the night!"

She was enthusiastic and very reassuring, so Tom and I looked at each other, shrugged and relaxed some. Meanwhile, she began to plan our visit with the others, quite pleased at the turn of events.

Each passenger settled into their preferred pastime, often dozing as the train labored south. When we arrived at Villa San Giovanni, life on the train stirred and a buzz filled the corridor and compartments. We could get off the train while the engineers disassembled it to load onto the ferry. We grabbed our valuables and followed the others out and up onto the upper deck to enjoy watching our approach to Sicily, always emotional for me. At about 6:00 P.M. the clouds were heavy and dark and the sun setting low in the west. Our nine to ten hour trip had already stretched into twelve hours. Once we were on our way again, we would still have about an hour and half journey before reaching Catania Centrale.

All went smoothly during the crossing and once in Sicily, at the port of Messina, the train was reassembled as we all filed back down to the hold and found our places, ready for the last leg of our journey. We arrived at Catania Centrale close to four hours late—getting from Catania to Pietraperzia still a niggling concern.

Meanwhile, Elena, Giovanni, and Damiana stayed close by us as we disembarked and looked around for our cousins, Elena promising over and over again a lovely evening as their guests.

"Please don't worry, my friends," she reminded us, "we will take care of you and not leave you alone in this unsafe city!" However, we were still hoping our cousins Vincenzo and Giacomo would be there, as tempting as an unexpected overnight stay at our new friends' home might seem. "We will call your cousins and help you arrange your onward journey," she thoughtfully added.

"Thank you so much," I responded. "That is very kind, but let's just head toward the terminal and perhaps meet my cousins along the way!"

"Of course," she agreed. All the others, Tom and Phil, Giovanni, Damiana and Laura trudged with us toward the station. At a certain point Laura found her brother who had come to pick her up. We all said goodbye as we embraced and watched her departure.

Perhaps our cousins also understand the train schedules better than we do and waited until a later hour to come for us I mused. We were all tired; my head was especially weary from trying to understand a strongly accented Italian all afternoon and to answer in barely decipherable Italian. *Traveling off the beaten track is not for sissies, whew . . .*

All of a sudden wonderful Vincenzo was there, reaching to embrace me with a smile and a tease, as he always did. "Maria, Tommaso, Filippo," he shouted! "Benvenuti (welcome)," he continued. His smile cancelled any doubts we might have had about returning again to visit the family. As the elder son of Zio Rocco, my grandmother's brother, Vincenzo represented the Zarba family protector, just as my Uncle Joe did in my childhood. Then Giacomo, the son of Salvatore, one of my grandmother's younger brothers, grabbed me and Tom and Phil with the same enthusiasm. We tried to explain circumstances, while Elena and her family assisted in adding copious details. We had a reunion right there still at the track before grabbing the suitcases again and continuing the necessary trek toward the terminal and the exit.

Elena was visibly disappointed that our family was there to meet us, and explained to them "We were hoping to take your cousins home with us and keep them safe!" The others in her party agreed, but, although affectionately grateful, we were thrilled by the arrival of our cousins. By then we were at the terminal and we had to say farewell. Again, embraces between everyone. Somehow we had all become just people, no longer Sicilians and Americans—just people. Nevertheless, we were very relieved to be on the way with our cousins Vincenzo and Giacomo to a party in our honor in Pietraperzia, complete with Tolaros and Zarbas. The Americans had again returned . . .

Figure 58. Women washing clothes in Pietraperzia

Figure 59. Panorama of Pietraperzia

Figure 60. Tom with Rocco Pagliaro trying on Tom's hat

Figure 61. Giacoma tagging along with Tom and the guidebook

Thomas and the Capricious Goats

This is one of the stories that bring our American and Sicilian families together in the telling, one of the first adventures together, and one of the reasons why we hold in such high esteem the friendly, capricious goats of the world.

Usually in August it does not rain in Sicily, especially in the center of the island where my family lives. The golden hills are arid and the fields are dry. Most flowers do not bloom and the air is hot and dry, the Scirocco winds often blowing over from North Africa. However, that August the clear blue sky frequently turned dark and menacing, and the storms rained down torrents. The roads in the countryside and the mountains were destroyed, with mud and rocks everywhere. The hail had ruined the peaches and ripe tomatoes waiting to be gathered and the grapes ready for the harvest. When we arrived on the seventh of August that year we found Sicily practically underwater.

Nevertheless, since we were American cousins, our family still thought that we should all go on a Sunday afternoon excursion to one of the provincial tourist destinations, in spite of the road warnings. They chose the Villa Romana del Casale, near Piazza Armerina, with its famous Roman mosaics. It was a cloudy, dark afternoon, and we were all hoping it would not rain. We went in two separate cars because there were eleven of us. Rocco, my cousin Nina's husband drove the first car, a new grey Alfa Romeo with Nina, their oldest daughter twelve-year-old Francesca, their two-year old twins Letizia and Emanuele, and Rocco's mother Francesca. Tom drove the other car, a tiny older black Fiat. Nina's mother Zia Giacoma, our son Philip, and little seven-year-old Giacoma, Nina and Rocco's other daughter, completed our group.

During the trip from Pietraperzia to Piazza Armerina we noticed two things. Rocco was driving very fast, and Tom had to as well because he had to follow Rocco, the only one who knew the way. In addition, we observed that because of the rain of the previous week, the little roads were ruined. Rocco chose the local route, not the autostrada, and the roads were hardly wide enough for pedestrians to pass. There were many dangerous curves and mud and rocks everywhere. To tell the truth, Tom was enjoying the drive, but was a little upset when the little car would bounce vigorously back and forth when he tried to shift from first to second gear. At every bounce, Zia Giacoma prayed the Our Father very fervently. She was quite afraid, as I was, holding on tightly to my seat, my knuckles turning white.

Instead little Giacoma giggled happily at the fun and Philip sat tranquilly, saying nothing, listening to his music with earphones and a Walkman, always the indifferent teenager. After about an hour we arrived at the Villa.

Our visit at the ancient ruins was fun for everyone, especially for us in company with locals. Now the site has been turned into a real tourist destination, but at that time it was still largely open and very disorganized. One could meander around and get very close to the pavements. Besides the mosaics, there were lots of late summer flowers. The puffy red spiny fruit of the fichidindia shrubs were maturing colorfully all around. I imagined myself enjoying a grand imperial dinner as I meandered around the site. Tom enjoyed elaborating on the historical aspects of the site in English, forgetting that hardly anyone could understand him. While Giacoma flitted around like a chatty butterfly "Zio, guarda," she'd say, "look at this flower!" Or "Zio look, look how high I can jump!"

Figure 62. Pagliaro Family, Piazza Armerina, 1990

Nina and Rocco chased after the twins while Francesca and Phil practiced conversing in rudimentary English and Italian. The two grandmothers walked arm in arm, smiling and gossiping in their dialect, probably about the frightful ride that Zia Giacoma had just experienced with the Americano. About an hour later, we all sat down on nearby rocks and ate homemade cookies with the twins Letizia and Emanuele.

At 6:30 we needed to leave the site because they were beginning to close the gates of the Villa, and the sun was setting. So we returned to the cars and started on our way back to Pietraperzia.

I hope that Tom remembers the way back, I thought, *and then we won't have to follow Rocco.* In fact, he did remember and we went on our way, much more calmly and safely than before. We lost sight of speedy Rocco, but no matter. Tom relaxed into his driving, Zia Giacoma chatted away in the dialect that I could hardly understand, little Giacoma tried to translate into Italian for me, and Phil listened to his music.

Sunset was fast approaching and the cloudy sky was full of every shade of orange. It was beautiful with the sun setting over the golden hills and trees, and over a day that also shimmered with the warm affection of a long-lost family finally together.

Suddenly Tom hit the breaks, startling us all and putting an end to my musings about the spectacular sunset and the warmth of family affection. None of us could believe our eyes!

"Look at all those goats," he exclaimed. Over a hundred lively goats unexpectedly crowded our narrow, muddy road. I covered my eyes in disbelief. The goats were everywhere, just like the rocks and the mud. Zia Giacoma was praying again. Little Giacoma laughed and chatted happily. (I didn't understand her though because, with my eyes closed, I couldn't understand Italian.) Although still calm, Phil was not listening to his music, but commenting on the situation in English. In other words, there was quite a cacophony of human voices accompanying the loud bleating of the goats.

Tom noticed that there was a bridge ahead, even narrower than the road. Meanwhile the goats were gallivanting briskly along, while the young goatherd tried to gather them together along the right side of the bridge so that the cars, namely ours, could pass.

Good idea!

However, a huge goat, as big as our little black Fiat, suddenly decided to cross the bridge and stand directly in front of us. Naturally, the other goats followed him. We had to stop because we were totally surrounded by capricious goats. What a traffic jam in remote Sicily!

Figure 63. Vincenzo di Cataldo sheparding goats as a boy, c. 1950

Our valiant driver had to "walk" the car ahead very slowly. The goats were yattering loudly, almost like us in the Fiat. Rocco and his passengers had disappeared from our view, of course.

What can one do in a moment like that? Behind us a long line of other cars had accumulated, their drivers impatient with our slow progress. When we arrived at the end of the bridge, Tom pulled ever to the side of the road to let the other cars pass. Meanwhile, the goats were all cavorting wildly here and there around us and the goatherd was trying to gather them together with his staff. His three Border Collies were barking at the goats with authority, while the goats were ignoring the shepherd, the dogs, and us.

All of a sudden we realized our little Fiat was sinking in the deep gooey mud. Meanwhile, while the driver of the car in back of us tried to pass us, Tom all of a sudden accelerated to escape from the goats. He forgot about the mud and the engine died as we sank deeper. He tried to start again, but the wheels just spun and dug deeper, and sprayed it all over everywhere.

The driver's side back window was wide open. Thankfully, the rear-view mirror managed to block the spraying mud from hitting our son's face as he was hanging out trying to see what was going on. Just then the driver of the other car hit the breaks and stopped all of a sudden and the sea of goats split up and ran off in all directions. The game was over, both for us and for the goats. We would never know what happened back there after our messy escape.

Then we picked up speed in order to find Rocco and the others. While Tom drove we heard the thick mud splatting from the wheel wells. Plop . . . plop . . . plop . . . plop—for kilometers.

Finally, after reuniting with the others, Rocco led us all to a gelateria to help us forget the ordeal: an inch or more of mud covered the left side of the car, the back of the rear-view mirror included; the driver was exhausted; the Zia was still praising the Lord for our salvation; a sixteen-year-old suddenly became lively and talkative; a young child was still very excited; and a signora (myself) was trying to remember all the details so she could write the story!

N.B. As luck would have it, the day after the above events, the town of Pietraperzia had no water because of a line break. Therefore, the thick mud baked on the Fiat for two sunny days. Finally, Rocco cleaned it but we could not even help because by then the cugini americani had gone off to Agrigento for a couple of days.

Buon Natale

Figure 64. Sketch of Christmas street scene, Pietraperzia

Once Upon a Time in December

Over time I have come to realize the happiness that memories add to my life. These are some of my sweetest recollections of one journey in early December 1995.

7 December 1995

"Ciao Zio," I said, maneuvering through the crowd of family squashed into Maria and Lillo's kitchen. "Here I am again, carissimo—the American has returned to Pietraperzia. What do you think of that?"

"Ma---ri-a," he exclaimed, "benvenuta." Ninety-one year-old Zio Rocco searched to deposit the container of hot coals he had been holding on his lap to stay warm, and then pressed himself up onto his feet with his cane. By that time I had reached him, having quickly hugged a few converging Zarba cousins as I had pushed through. His arms opened up wide in welcome and the wooden cane crashed to the floor with no hand to hold it. We embraced, and he began his usual litany of loving greetings to me and, through me, to all of his American family, exulting in the joy of my surprise visit.

"Thank you for coming. You surprised me. Thank you, thank you. How is my nephew Filippo, your father? And your dear mother, Rita? Tommaso, how is Tommaso? When will your husband come again? Thank you for the letters and cards. Thank them too. Thank you for the gifts. I can't write to you myself and I worry that I can't thank you. Someone has to write for me and . . . thank you. But thank you for always returning. Thank you ... thank you ... the joy ... the joy ... I can't tell you the joy ..."

I hung there in his arms for what seemed a long time, soaking up the warmth of his affection as he continued to chant softly in my ear, the cadence of the Sicilian dialect finally familiar, and even soothing. The tickle of his breath as it flashed by triggered, as it always does, the memory of our very first embrace six years earlier, at the Albergo Di Prima in Caltanissetta, when my journey had barely begun . . .

I had decided at the last minute to make a surprise visit to my family in Pietraperzia before returning home to California. I had been studying Italian in Bologna for two months and needed a big family hug. I was still not used to traveling alone and spending so much time among strangers. Besides, I had thought, I can see how much my Italian has improved. Perhaps I will finally be able to have a meaningful conversation with Zio Rocco. That had always been my goal in continuing my studies—a conversation with my grandmother's brother. Although he only spoke the local dialect, he could understand me if I spoke decent Italian.

The visit was gratifying because of my growing ability to communicate, not only with my uncle, but also with the rest of the family. We would get together at someone's house on the cold, damp evenings and eat a light cena. All of the generations would then clear the table and bring out playing cards and board games, and the evening would evolve into a teasing fest and an opportunity for me to feel truly immersed. Generally, I am not a game player, but those evenings were memorable because of the closeness and affection that surrounded me during that trip, the closeness and affection they felt toward each other, but also toward me.

I remembered that same kind of evening when I was growing up in Bellows Falls, evenings at either my grandparents' house or at one of the other family homes. The teasing uncles thrilled us children by their attention—even though Uncle Jim was always trying to cheat at cards. Actually our cousin Vincenzo Zarba, who played the same pranks on those cold December evenings in Pietraperzia, reminded me a lot of his American cousin. And the Family Circle expands ...

9 December 1995

"Zia, zia, vieni qui, guarda," beckoned seven-year-old Emanuele as soon as Nina released the door to let me in. He grabbed my hand and pulled me into the tiny living room/dining room and pointed excitedly at the decorated Christmas tree standing up on a table, reigning over the family space. It was always fun to visit that branch of the Tolaro family. My cousin Nina, daughter of my grandfather's first cousin Giovanni, and her husband Rocco Pagliaro, have four children, and their house is always full of activity and commotion. I was there for pranzo and had arrived early to help, or play with my young cousins. Emanuele would have actually preferred my husband Tom as a companion, since he's more fun. That day though, I would suffice. With me in tow, he dashed over to an ordinary cardboard box and started dumping its contents onto the already-set table, including the pulverized chunks of what appeared to be mud.

Figure 65. With Tolaros and Pagliaros in Pietraperzia, Sicily

"Emanuele," I squealed, the Italian sliding more easily from my lips at last. I hurriedly pushed the figurines back into the box. "These are beautiful. But I think we had better look at them on the floor. Aren't you hungry? We don't want to mess up the table, do we? Tell me what they are, please?" In the meantime, I had greeted the rest of the family—Nina, his mother; Francesca, outgoing, grown-up, the oldest at seventeen; beautiful, timid Giacoma, thirteen; Letizia, seven, her huge almost-black eyes full of mischief like her twin's. The normal commotion of a typical family continued as pranzo was being prepared and the television blared, totally ignored.

Emanuele and I sat on the floor together and he began his exuberant explanation of the box's contents, which lay on the floor between us. "Zia, these are the pastorelli–aren't they bea-u-ti-ful?" he exclaimed? "Do you have these at your house in America?" I fingered the worn, plastic figurines as he handed them to me, noting that each one depicted a different artisan. The muscled shepherd slung a sheep over his shoulders, walking toward someplace. The bread maker stood smiling broadly beside the cave of his wood oven, a finished loaf of bread lying on the paddle he extended to someone as a gift. The water bearer, a woman with a huge ceramic jar on her head, balanced by the curve of her strong, but slender arms, promised to sashay forward with graceful ease, while singing a simple song.

"Sì, Emanuele," I said finally, "these are truly beautiful. No, I don't have any of them at home. Please explain them to me? What are you going to do with them? Are they your toys?"

"No," he answered, reverently, "No, zia, these we will put under the Christmas tree. They will welcome Jesus. They will all go to the stable to welcome Jesus, and they will bring him gifts—don't you see?" He held out the shepherd, and grabbed the butcher lying there next to him.

Just then Zia Giacoma, Emanuele's grandmother who lives upstairs, appeared in the doorway, and he jumped up to greet her while I pushed myself up more slowly from my position on the floor. Zio Giovanni's wife, a widow since his death two years before, radiated affection as her expressive eyes jumped out to connect with mine. Our two cheeks touched in greeting, first the left, then the right, and then she grabbed me for a serious hug. "Maria," she said, "do you remember the first time you came with your mother and father, and then Tommaso arrived with your sons?"

I stood there with her, our hands still pressing, emotions of the past and present linking us. "Yes, Zia, I remember . . . and I remember how much you wanted to communicate with us. I tried to understand. I tried so hard, but it was impossible. And I remember how you tried even harder than we did. You never stopped trying to explain everything to us, to welcome us, and I remember how you grew so frustrated and would talk faster and louder, hoping that you could force your meaning into our spinning brains."

She shook her head in agreement, her thoughts obviously on the past. Then we finally noticed Emanuele's impatient pleas for attention.

"Come here zia. I have to explain everything to you," he shouted. "I wasn't finished, come here, please. You come too, nonna."

"Emanuele," his mother warned as she took a break from cooking in the kitchen to greet her mother. "Leave your zia alone, let her visit with nonna. And why did you dump the whole box of pastorelli out onto the floor?" she added. But Emanuele had launched back into his demonstration of the figures, and without warning Zia Giacoma pulled me back over to where Emanuele sat. She grabbed a handful of the figures and carried them with her to the couch. She seemed transported again to another place, another time, as she looked at each one.

"Oh look, Maria . . . Maria . . . look. Here they are, the pastorelli." By that time, Rocco had arrived with a big metal bucket that he set down as he greeted me. All the children hurried to glance into the bucket and the excitement began to grow. I didn't know what was going on, but when I looked into the container and saw it full of clumps of sod, moss and even a small plant or two, I was even more confused.

"Now we can put them under the tree," shouted Emanuele, as he jumped up, forgetting me, and everything else. Evidently, his father held the secret to being ready. Nina returned again and assigned Francesca the task of blanketing the cut Christmas tree's underside with the still fragrant earth and ordered her son to pick up the figures and put them in the box so that the family could move around in the cramped space. Francesca, with the help of Giacoma, arranged the thick, moist earth just so and I helped Emanuele pick up the figures. Letizia, his twin jumped up and down, anxious to get started, "Hurry, hurry," she said, eyes sparkling with excitement. We lugged the box up to the nearest chair and Zia Giacoma pushed over next to me.

"Now Maria," she said, all at once her dancing eyes matching those of her seven-year-old granddaughter Letizia "do you know the story of il Signore?" Without waiting for my reply, she suddenly began to sing, her sweet, thin, almost childlike voice recounting their traditional Christmas story—the journey of Mary and Joseph, the search for lodging, the meager stable, the birth of the Christ Child, the star in the heavens, the angels and then, what she had been getting to all along, the shepherds and the townspeople that came to adore him. She dug through the box as she sang and looked with pleasure while she held each shepherd, waterbearer, baker, fisherman . . . caressing it lovingly, not only with her hands, but also with her eyes. Each seemed costly bone china or Murano glass by her demeanor. Then she handed the piece to Francesca or Giacoma to place carefully under the tree, surrounded by the earth of the campagna. Her singing riveted even Emanuele, who stood next to me, his eyes glued to his grandmother's face as she sang, then to her expressive hands as she passed each figure to one of his big sisters, then to their hands as they transferred it to its place under the tree.

Figure 66. Tolaro family Christmas, North Walpole, 1953

Her song told of the journey each had taken to find the stable, the star they had followed, the gift each had brought, no matter how meager, and the joy each had found upon arrival at the destination.

I stood there, not only listening and watching my Sicilian family, but actually a part of the goings on, and finally, the journey of the last six years of my life made sense to me—my passion to learn Italian, the hunger to be with them as often as possible. As I had ventured out, in search of my roots, I had actually traveled deeper into my own heart and found myself. The gift I had brought to them was reconnecting to the family they had thought lost. Among the gifts I had received in return though, besides their affection and welcoming warmth, was the wonder of listening to my own heart. In the joy of that December day in Pietraperzia I glimpsed the promise of tomorrow.

One Saturday in May

My grandmother made sure that we grew up revering one of Pietra-perzia's principal patrons, the Madonna della Cava. The story recalls the Madonna, a cave, a miracle, and a young mute boy from Trapani.

"Viva Maria Santissima della Cava!" The image of Maria SS Della Cava was rediscovered miraculously in the year 1223 by the young Trapanese who had been directed by Our Lady in a dream to proceed to the outskirts of Pietraperzia where the icon would be found in one of the caves. He succeeded on the third attempt. His speech and hearing were miraculously restored, and his first words proclaimed the Blessed Mother's sanctity.

The Pietrini who had immigrated in the early twentieth century to Boston, would gather and celebrate this most revered patron of their hometown at a huge festival and procession in the North End in August, around the time of the Assumption celebrated on August 15. In my house in California I have one of my grandparents' framed prints remembering the event there years ago.

I never went to the procession and festival in Boston's Little Italy, but one Saturday in May in the late 1990s, the month that celebrates the Madonna in the Catholic ecclesiastical calendar, I did find myself in Pietraperzia, participating in a procession and festa organized by the *carrettieri* or cart drivers of the village. Zio Rocco was still alive and co-starred, to a certain extent, in the celebratory events of the day. He was the oldest living *carrettiere* and the Grand Marshall of the procession from the town out to the Sanctuary, about 2.5 miles away.

Zio Rocco was especially pleased at the honor being bestowed on him. He looked forward to his role of Grand Marshall and riding in the brightly painted and restored Sicilian cart with his son Vincenzo, who had also been a *carrettiere* in his youth. An elaborate banner of the Madonna della Cava from the town would be carried in homage to the Sanctuary in the countryside. He would be on the most beautiful lead cart, pulled by an exuberant, prancing white stallion festooned with brilliant red, yellow, blue, and green feathers and ribbons to match the colors of the painted cart.

Pilgrims have come for centuries to pay homage to the patron, to request their own personal miracle, or perhaps to thank the Madonna for a previous grace received. The custom is to walk barefoot from the town to the Sanctuary on a Saturday while reciting the rosary. Often the church is the site of important rites and the grounds and additional buildings the place of local celebrations.

On that day the *carrettieri* were honoring the Madonna, just as other groups would honor her on other Saturdays. Since the area around Pietraperzia has been considered farming territory over the course of history, the cart drivers with their elaborately painted carts would bring the products to the cities and return with passengers and city goods to the paese. According to tradition, the workers would have been praying to the Madonna for a good growing season so that their transportation business would thrive. For generations the Zarba family had been *carrettieri* and Zio Rocco was both his family's and the town's oldest living representative.

The day was sunny and the warmth of spring had allowed the early flowers to bloom, the trees to wake up and the green leaves and colorful buds to burst open and brighten the town's greyness. The family festivities actually began at pranzo, with a large contingent of the Zarba family congregating at Damiana's house to eat the midday meal together. Zio Rocco lived with his daughter at the time. He was of course at the head of the table and proudly holding court. A short, slight figure in his late 90s, he was the cherished head of the family.

During pranzo many toasts were offered to his health and long life and his broad smile expressed the pleasure of the day. He was one of the sweetest, mildest, most loving people I have ever known. I only saw him angry once when we were all spending an August at the house in the campagna and he was swinging his wooden cane and cursing at the circling family dogs that were trying to steal his food. He always dressed the same, whether at the table, watching TV, or out visiting other family members: a suitable plaid sport shirt according to the season, a soft wool sweater vest, and a tweedy sport coat. I do not ever remember seeing him without his cap both in the house and outside—the traditional berretta of the region, flat with an almost hidden front brim.

That Saturday in May he was also very pleased that I was there to participate in the festivities and see him lead the procession. He told me, "Maria, we *carrettieri* had a very difficult life, always on the road regardless of the weather and the season. It was our only work.

We did not eat if we did not work and our families would starve." Even the children had to help. They were very poor, but proud, and the dilapidated family *carretto* still reposed in the garage at Vincenzo's house because his father would not part with it.

Figure 67. Zio Rocco in carter's procession, c. 1990s

The town was full of excitement that day because of the anticipated afternoon festivities. We cleaned up after pranzo while Zio Rocco rested and in mid-afternoon Vincenzo arrived to accompany his father to the starting position of the procession, outside of Santa Maria di Gesù in Piazza Garibaldi, the town's main piazza. We all made our way there as well and arrived along with just about everyone else in the town: young and old alike, the teenagers especially thrilled to have an excuse to hang out together and walk arm in arm along the route, and joke and flirt and tease. The elderly signoras formed another contingent, dressed solemnly in black with rosary beads at the ready for the beginning of the procession when Father Bongiovanni would lead the prayers. Young families and large extended families were there, as were both of mine, waiting to begin the walk. The horses were hitched up to the long line of colorful *carretti* that had arrived from all over the region to participate. The bands were lining up and tuning their instruments, everyone waiting happily impatient to get started. Many of the elderly gentlemen would not join the walk, but were parading around the piazza observing and commenting on the goings-on.

I was very excited to be there—pleased to experience another aspect of my grandparents' life. My grandmother used to describe the event to me and there I was, ready to live the modern version with all the Tolaro and Zarba cousins surrounding me and my uncle, her brother, the Grand Marshall! My heart was full of thanks and joy that day.

Zio Rocco arrived and was carried up to the seat arranged for him on the cart. He waved at all of us there below him and smiled, the happiest I had ever seen him. The parade began with the band and the town functionaries leading the way and we all walked along beside his *carretto*, as the immense white horse hitched to the *carretto* eagerly pulled forward and began his trek. I walked arm in arm with my cousin Damiana among the host of other Zarbas. Along the way we met up with my other cousins, the Tolaros, and stopped to embrace and chat and tease the children, who were excited and waiting for the promised gelato once we arrived at the Sanctuary. Even though it was Saturday, everyone was dressed in his or her Sunday best, and the mood was more festive than solemn and religious, at least around us.

When we got to the Sanctuary the *carretti* were all parked and horses tended to and then the photograph taking began. With Zio Rocco proudly sitting on top, next to his son Vincenzo, I took one of my favorite photographs. That evening while discussing the events of the day over cena, Zio Rocco said to me, "Now Maria, don't believe all of the fancy show they put on today. I never had a elegant white horse to pull my cart—we had a mule, a very slow stubborn mule, and it was very hard work!"

Figure 68. Dad and Vincenzo, holding Zio Rocco's *carretto*

Figure 69. Zio Rocco, Grand Marshall of Cart Drivers' Procession

The Soul of Pietraperzia

During Holy Week, Grandma would describe with both pride and melancholy the evocative procession of Good Friday in Pietraperzia: Lu Signuri di li Fasci.

A mountain of white linen bands floated like a sail against an indigo sky over a dark gentle sea. Cries of "Pietà, Misericordia, Signuri!" punctuated the chilly night and echoed off the ancient stone palazzos as my cousin Damiana and I followed behind the solemn cortège. We were part of an immense crowd—townspeople, returning sons and daughters, and foreign visitors—snaking slowly through the narrow streets of the town on Good Friday evening: *Lu Signuri di li Fasci a Pietraperzia.* I was finally there. I felt like a tiny speck in a sea of emotionally charged humanity.

Through her stories, my grandmother Maria Calogera had transformed the rituals and procession of Good Friday in Pietraperzia into an otherworldly affair in an enchanted land. When she described her native town's principle religious procession, her eyes would take on an absent look and she seemed far away for just an instant.

"Now, Mary Alice," she would say. She always began her stories and admonitions that way. As she created a little cross for me with the blessed palm frond from the previous Palm Sunday's church service, she would continue "You remember that Jesus died on the cross for our sins on Good Friday. In Pietraperzia we had a long procession that took all night. Many men carried a very heavy cross, covered with a canopy and balanced by the townspeople holding on to strips of white linen. And His Mother would be carried along too, crying because of what they did to her Son." My grandmother was the mother of eight children; her heart always suffered with the grieving Madonna, the Addolorata.

I had arrived a few days earlier to the welcoming embrace of my Tolaro and Zarba relatives, anxious to live first hand the events related to Holy Week and Easter. It took no time to get caught up in the buzz and energy of Holy Week, with at least one event or religious service to attend each day. In the meantime though, the topic of the procession on Good Friday always surfaced in the conversation.

On that Good Friday afternoon the church of the Carmine was overflowing with townspeople and visitors, a combination of solemnity and excitement filling the space. I crowded into the pew along with Tolaro cousins, the young ones squirming and whispering, waiting for the service to begin. Finally, at 3:00 the chant "Pietà, Misericordia, Signuri!" rang out in the clipped cadence of the local dialect, halting the quiet hum of conversation. The yearly ritual had officially started. At that instant when I first experienced its beginning—when "Compassion, Mercy, O Lord!" became the chant of what seemed like the entire town's population—that day brought me back into my grandparents' flowery wallpapered bedroom in their house in North Walpole looking up at the crucifix centered over their bed, following the gestures and words of my grandmother as she related the story of Christ and His Mother.

The *governatore*, or president of the *Confraternity of the SS. Maria del Soccorso* (Confraternity of the Blessed Mother of Salvation), climbed up the portable stairway placed against the wall, just high enough to reach the revered fourteenth century crucifix (~4 feet/120 cm.), and removed it with white-gloved hands from its glass case. He was dressed, as were the other members of the brotherhood, in a white cassock and arm length blue cape trimmed in gold braid. He wore a white veil, which covered the top of his head and was secured back behind at the neck. As he cradled the crucifix, he kissed the figure of Christ and passed it down to the next confraternity member and again cried "Pietà, Misericordia, Signuri!" The crucifix traveled in that manner to other confraternity members, arriving at a six-foot long antique wooden cross, laid horizontally on a red-draped platform. The figure was mounted ceremoniously on the cross, ready to receive the homage of the faithful until the evening program.

The members of the *Confraternity of the SS. Maria del Soccorso* had been preparing all day for the afternoon service and the evening procession. They directed young and old as they filed past the cross. A confraternity brother would touch a *misuredda*, a red ribbon cut to the size of the arm breadth of the crucified Christ and hand it to the passing individual, who would kiss it. The ribbon is a symbol of the suffering of Christ and the measure of God's love for us. It is tied to the arm and worn to symbolize the individual's sorrow for His suffering and death. I too passed by, accompanied by Nina, Zia Giacoma and all the children and grandchildren. Our family was only one in an overwhelming crowd of spiritually charged adults and exuberant young people and little ones.

Perhaps one of the most evocative moments during the afternoon service was the initial chanting of the *ladata*, an acapella song of lamentation in the town's dialect, which remembers the passion and death of Christ. A small group of men stood in a circle facing each other. Three solo voices and a small choral group sang each verse in a minor key, a sorrowful, wailing cry, narrating each episode of the Passion. The *ladata* would continue later that night at various moments along the "Way of the Cross" until the end of the procession.

In the late afternoon I headed over to Damiana's house. She had offered to accompany me that evening as I experienced every aspect of *Lu Signuri di li Fasci*. We left for the church of the Carmine about 7:30 p.m.

Figure 70. Families holding their *fascia* once attached

At 8:00 when dusk was settling in, we were there in the *piazzetta* outside the church, along with what seemed like the whole town and plenty of visitors. German, English, Italian, and the local dialect all mixed together in a jumble that made Pietraperzia seem like the center of the world. Meanwhile members of the brotherhood exited the church with the huge hull-like base. They placed it on its side. Next the cross itself (~28-foot/8.5 meters tall, including the base), made of cypress wood, was transported into the piazza and inserted into the base of what would become the enormous structure. It resembled a huge ship's mast. A metal ring, consisting of two semicircles was affixed to the shaft near the top and the long process of attaching the white linen fasciae began. The fasciae are each 16-inches/40 cm. wide and 110 feet/33 meters long. Normally initials embroidered in red of the original proprietor along with the inaugural year mark each one. The canopy evolved slowly as roughly 200 individual white linen bands were folded in half and tied to the metal ring. Two members of each participating family, 400 in all, would grasp one of the two ends of their linen strip and, following the instructions of the confraternity brothers, maneuver the canopy allowing it to rotate, turn corners, expand, and compress according to the requirements of the route.

Once the fasciae were all secured and verified safe, a wood-framed globe with facets of deep red, blue, green, and gold glass arrived and was affixed to the mast, just above the metal ring and bands. Since 1888 the globe was fastened to the mast under the crucifix to symbolize the diversity of the world.

Another *passamano* began, as the crucifix was passed from the church of the Carmine, from one brother's hands to the next, each one repeating the same "Pietà, Misericordia, Signuri!" Still the silence held as the Christ figure was attached to the cross at the very top over the globe. A hush as the crowd waited . . . two beats of the hammer on the wood block by the *Mastro di Vara* . . . a deep inhale, a gasp and, at the third resonant beat . . . the entire structure slowly rose up into position, like the launch of a giant sailing ship. The three beats of the hammer on the wood is said to remember the three inflictions of Christ nailed to the cross. Meanwhile, a rush of activity followed as the 400 individuals managing the fasciae pulled, pushed, and repositioned the canopy at the direction of confraternity members.

The padded crossbeams that would be carried on the shoulders of 80 of the town's young men were attached and then the procession of Venerdì Santo, Good Friday in Pietraperzia began. A glass casket with a life-sized figure of the crucified Christ inside exited the church on a platform strewn with pink, purple, and white flowers. The platform rested on the shoulders of a group of young men and followed behind the immense cross structure. A slow dirge of the local marching band accompanied the white mountain of fasciae as it made its way slowly floating out of the *piazzetta* on the shoulders of the townspeople, down toward Santa Maria Maggiore; some have even suggested that the canopy itself symbolizes Mount Calvary and, in fact, early historical notes suggest the original name of the procession was "Lu Calvaniu" or "The Calvary." At the Matrice, the statue of the Madonna Addolorata, carried on the shoulders of the women members of the *Associazione Maria SS. Addolorata* joined the cortège. They wore dark blue robes and white veils over their heads and shoulders. The sweet voices of the women sang a hymn filled with the sadness of a mother's grief and another marching band joined the procession.

The procession began and ended in the piazza outside of the church of the Carmine and lasted about five hours, including numerous rest stops for those carrying the heavy life-sized statues on their flower decorated platforms and for those managing the linen bands. The *Mastro di Vara* beat a block of wood again two times to signal a stop and then three times to signal the resumption of the journey. At each stop along the "Way of the Cross" another verse of the *ladata* was sung marking another moment in Christ's Passion. The phrase "Pietà, Misericordia, Signuri!" continued to ring out during the entire march.

Directly in front of the massive mountain of white, the members of the confraternity led the procession, and the rest of us followed behind, alongside, or in between the other floats and marching bands. While the initial religious rites were generally characterized by silence and spirituality, the evolving procession became loudly social and party-like for a majority of the people: Some of us were family members of fasciae holders, ready for the switch off; some of us were mothers of band members, offering water and snacks to the marchers; some of us were friends there to tease and joke with the participants or to offer encouragement; some of us were praying, our rosary beads dangling from folded hands; and some of us were soaking up the spiritual atmosphere of family, friendship, and tradition.

Damiana and I participated for the duration of the procession. When I look back to 1989 and our first visit to Pietraperzia, I realize that Zio Rocco's daughter has always been by my side, loving in her acceptance of her American cousin and generous in her encouragement. Besides that, she is beautiful like her aunt Maria Calogera, always smiling when she speaks and ready to accept me. Sharing the evening with her was perfect. We started out arm in arm, ready for the long march on a chilly evening since Easter was early that year. I remember silence during the religious moments and friendly banter along the way. Damiana and I both have countless family members in the town and everyone was out. We met her children and grandchildren, the other Zarbas—Giacomo and Rosetta for sure—and all of the Tolaros as well. Massimo and Vincenzo Zarba were holding the family fasciae in thanks for the birth of Vincenzo's new daughter and I took my turn too. Nina and Rocco Pagliaro were there with their children, plus many grandchildren running around, not so patiently awaiting the stop at the bar for the hot chocolate treat. Letizia and Emanuele, the now twin "Twenty-Somethings," were socializing with their friends, but took time to stop for a greeting and an embrace. I met Zia Giacoma Tolaro's sister again as they passed us, arm in arm too, absolutely thrilled with the evening's excitement and the "Americana" among them. My emotions were running high, joy at the top. We stopped twice with Damiana's many friends that we met along the way for a cup of hot tea, and to rest.

Figure 71. The grieving Madonna following the crucified Christ

At the intersection of Viale della Pace and Via Stefano di Blasi, the midpoint of the procession, the canopy had to be turned around—a very complicated process that required those holding the fasciae to reposition quickly, without running into each other, the walls of the adjacent buildings, or allowing the mast to become unbalanced. Once accomplished, the more challenging march back up the hill toward Santa Maria Maggiore and the church of the Carmine began.

That night we arrived back at the Carmine about 1:30 a.m., tired and satisfied. Those carrying the canopy and crucifix were visibly exhausted, as were those manning the linen bands. Our number was greatly reduced at the late hour and the atmosphere quiet and somber. The process of deconstructing the structure began. Three beats of the hammer on the wood block signaled the slow lowering of the mast, which landed gently into the upstretched hands of the waiting confraternity brothers. Once the fasciae were removed, rolled from each end into two large spools, and handed to the waiting family, the remainder of the process was carried out by the confraternity and we headed home, tired and anticipating the experiences that the next few days would offer: Easter and especially Pasquetta in the countryside on Monday.

**Figure 72. Old print of the procession of Good Friday,
Pietraperzia, c. 1600**

114

After my experience at the *Lu Signuri di li Fasci* in Pietraperzia that year, I finally realized, even after many previous visits to my paternal grandparents' hometown, that the procession truly personifies the town's heart and soul. Because of my family, both American and Sicilian, I was not merely a spectator, but also a loving participant. Thank you ...

Figure 73. Mary and Marisa, at Ausilia's wedding, Agrigento, 1995

The Signora Americana

My stories are fewer now. They often revolve around other visits to other destinations on the island. The following one happened in September 2013, just when I was feeling like a pro because of my years of exploring and the breadth of my experience. The kindness of the Sicilian people never ceases to amaze me though, and the possibility to have another Sicilian adventure urges me onward, with my family happily involved as well.

As he maneuvered the bus around mountainous curves on the road into Caltanissetta, the driver shouted: "Signora Americana, I have just spoken with the driver of the bus going to Pietraperzia." I startled, suddenly alert—he was addressing me . . .

For twenty-four years I had been traveling from Palermo to Pietraperzia, using a variety of public means, usually the bus, and experience has taught me that I must always verify scheduling and route changes first. I had done it and been informed earlier by the official ticket agent at the station that a reasonable connection at Caltanissetta would get me to my destination. However, sometimes I forget that Sicily is always Sicily and no matter how well I organize myself, surprises will come along . . . thus, I continue to have adventures along the way, and a story too. Caltanissetta often seems to be part of the adventure, remembering my very first experience in June 1989 with my parents and our monstrous rented van, the White Whale. At least this last time I was not the driver and I could understand Italian reasonably well and speak it passably. However ...

Palermo Bus Station in Via P. Balsamo – Chaos

So, with ticket in hand I waited for the appointed bus. The scene was constant chaos. Buses zipped onto the one-way street, picked up passengers, and zipped out. There were two lanes of parked buses and one lane open for traffic to pass through. Buses came, buses went. Usually they had a sign in the front window that stated the final destination. No one announced arrivals and departures, let alone destinations. Besides the traffic confusion there were of course various crowds of passengers, street hawkers, suspicious loiterers eyeing bags, foreigners from around the world, small town visitors from villages near and far, and savvy commuters. I watched the designated parking spot for my bus fully aware that it is only a suggestion and the bus could be boarding anywhere along the chaotic street.

As the departure time approached, I asked bus drivers milling about, getting in their last smoke before beginning their runs, which bus would be heading to Caltanissetta? The answer was generally "could be the one parked there, but to keep verifying." I did. By this time a number of fellow passengers were beginning to worry and actually treated me as the "go to" expert. We became a team and eventually found the right bus in the middle of the pack and, after putting our bags underneath in the hold, got in line to board.

Uh, oh ...

I handed the driver my ticket, with Pietraperzia the destination. He looked at me and stopped the routine punching of the paper tickets, and insisted, "But signora there is no connection in Caltanissetta at the appropriate time. You will have to wait hours there for a ride. You will be stuck, so do not take this bus."

Ever the logical, optimistic American, I answered, "But the ticket agent assured me that there would be one."

"Well, signora, she was wrong, so you had better just stay here."

"I'll at least get to Caltanissetta, sir."

"A very bad idea, signora. You will need a miracle ... even if we manage to leave soon and arrive there early to catch the one you will miss."

"I can contact my cousins if necessary, sir," as I held my ticket there for him to punch.

He gave me that look that says "What a dumb American lady!" and handed me my validated ticket with a glare. I moved down the aisle and took a seat on the opposite side, a few rows back. A nice gentleman, who had asked me for advice before boarding, smiled from his seat a row back and opposite mine. He seemed concerned, friendly, and empathetic.

The bus driver, meanwhile, continued to board the passengers, glancing every once in awhile at me as I sat there watching him. His intensely blue eyes were lively, and he engaged everyone, with a joke or comment to share. He was short and handsome, dressed officially in a dark blue v-neck sweater with a blue-grey tie. The thick brush of a salt and pepper crew cut topped his suntanned rectangular face. He seemed to like his job. I'm optimistic.

On the Road to Caltanissetta – Pause

I gathered my thoughts, worried, but just a little. I watched our time as we traveled along SLOWLY through the streets of Palermo. There was talk of some kind of a transit strike, as usual. About 45 minutes into the trip I decided to call my cousin Nina and advise her of my problem getting a bus to Pietraperzia. I was still optimistic. I told her I would let her know if I needed a ride, but not to worry. I could wait if no one was readily available to fetch me.

When I knew we were getting close to Caltanissetta, I checked my watch and saw that we were late, so I would need a ride to Pietraperzia. No big deal. Other passengers were starting to wake up and chat and the bus driver was actually fiddling with his cell phone making a call. I remember thinking how unsafe it seemed, but . . . Sicilia! After a heated conversation with someone on the other end, he went back to driving for five minutes or so. Probably making lunch plans, I mused.

Figure 74. Vincenzo and Dad harvesting grapes, 1992

Back to the Beginning

As he maneuvered the bus around mountainous curves on the road into Caltanissetta, the driver shouted: "Signora Americana, I have just spoken with the driver of the bus going to Pietraperzia." I startled, suddenly alert—*he was addressing me.*

And at that instant my phone rang. It was my cousin Nina in Pietraperzia. I responded but asked her to hold on a second while the bus driver continued shouting his message to all of us on the bus. "Signora Americana, I have just arranged with my colleague to meet us at a certain spot, and to wait if necessary." He was very pleased with himself, his ice-blue eyes staring up into the huge rear view mirror directly at me in my seat half a dozen rows back on his right. I didn't know what to say, so just responded "mille grazie, molto gentile." However, he continued to explain his plan. He had told the other driver to look for an American signora in a red blouse who needed to get to Pietraperzia. Meanwhile, I thanked him profusely and the bus erupted in applause for his kindness to the poor foreign lady as I then tried to explain to Nina what had happened, not to worry, and I would let her know when I was on my way and had a more precise time for my arrival in Pietraperzia. Evidently, the other passengers had been worrying about me too and they were all smiling, commenting about my situation. The hospitality of the Sicilian people helped me to never feel alone in my solitude. I was not in Caltanissetta yet though, let alone Pietraperzia . . .

A short time later he pulled over to the side of the road, a turn off of sorts. We were on a downward curve going around a high hill. Cars were parked there. A couple of other passengers got off too and went to their parked car or to a waiting car. I got off and thanked the bus driver. He was beaming, very pleased with himself. As I exited he added, "Signora, go up that hill behind us. You will find a parking lot where the other bus driver will be waiting for you at the appropriate bus stop."

"Mille grazie," I responded, certain that all was going to work out well thanks to him, in spite of his brusque admonitions when I had checked in on the bus that morning. Optimistic, I went to retrieve my luggage from the hold under the bus.

Somewhere in Caltanissetta – Friendly Encounters

I rolled my suitcase up the hill with my full backpack on my shoulders. I could see nothing until I got past the curve. Yes! There was a parking lot! I had understood the directions!!!! *Whew ... but darn this traveling with all the books, computer, etc.*

I entered the parking lot and recognized it as the usual transfer point on previous trips. Numerous shabby bus shelters with dilapidated signs overflowed with carousing high school students. The signs did not give a destination though. I first noticed a group of young men who were playing loud music and pushing each other around in jest. I decided to search out a less boisterous group to interrupt. I spotted a couple of young women chatting at a stop that had no shelter and figured they might be able to tell me where to wait for the bus to Pietraperzia. Meanwhile, no buses were in sight. I went up to them and they were shy and very polite. As it turned out they needed the same bus! I was in luck.

They informed me, very concerned though, that perhaps the bus would not show up. Sometimes one did, other times no. One never knew. I explained to them that evidently one would stop that day because my bus driver from Palermo had spoken with the bus driver, who was planning to pick me up. They were thrilled with the information and I felt very pleased to give them good news.

So we waited and chatted. Meanwhile more kids showed up and the parking lot suddenly exploded in animated antics particular to teenagers everywhere. Suddenly buses started pulling into the lot one after the other, hardly waiting for the students to get on. Rush, rush, rush. Thank goodness I had my two companions and a couple of others that had shown up in the meantime. We were all searching for the little sign in the front corner of the windshield that indicated the destination.

Hopes Dashed

Nina called again. While we were talking a bus came in with Pietraperzia on the sign! We all cheered—but it didn't stop. It just sped by, the driver not even glancing our frantic way. So I told her that in fact the bus just drove by us without stopping so they had better come and get me. I told her I would meet them at the entrance of the parking lot and indicated it was not the main terminal lot, but the one where the Pietraperzia bus picked up the high school students.

Figure 75. Rocco Pagliaro and Nina Tolaro, 2007

So, I gathered my stuff and bid the young women goodbye and wished them luck getting home. I explained that my cousin would come to get me and I needed to move to a more visible location. I trundled off dodging the groups of students still waiting around.

I waited patiently, realizing it would probably take a half hour or so for them to arrive. In the meantime buses continued to enter the lot and pick up one group or another of students. After about ten minutes of waiting the two young women came out to where I was standing. The bus driver who had spoken with my friend the Palermo bus driver had arrived and he was looking for me "la signora Americana con la camicia rossa." So I ran with all my stuff back there to the bus stop and talked to the bus driver, thanking him and the girls for their assistance. I explained that now my cousins were on the way and I needed to wait for them outside the gate. Everyone was very disappointed that I would not be joining them, but I shook the driver's hand and embraced the young women and ran back to my spot outside the gate.

Then the Fun Began

I was by myself on the sidewalk at the gate of the parking lot. In the meantime all the students had been picked up by the last flood of buses and left me alone with parked cars in the lot, and not even traffic on the road outside. I decided to venture from the corner spot and look up the hill, just in case I could see a street sign or something to give me a sense of place. Nothing. Just a bit of sidewalk, and no signs, some trees and bushes across the street on the side of the hill. That was it. *Where are Nina and Rocco? They should have been here by now.* We had last spoken more than a half hour ago.

My phone rang again. It was Rocco. "Where in the world are you," he asked? "We are at the bus depot and we can't find you."

I, of course answered, as matter-of-factly as possible, "Just as I explained before, I'm not at the main bus terminal, but outside the parking lot where the buses pick up the high school students to bring them to their various home towns." Actually, I believe it's the previous main bus depot, where I had been deposited and picked up for twenty years. "Where is it? he asked. "Give me some point of reference." I answered honestly when I said "I have absolutely no idea where I am . . ." I suggested he ask someone there at the terminal. He said okay and hung up.

I was still hopeful that they would find me. Someone there at the main terminal must know how the local transportation system works. How am I supposed to know?

I waited another fifteen minutes and nothing, till the next phone call. Rocco was quite agitated now and said he had gotten no help and was totally puzzled about my whereabouts and without a clue as to what to do. "Ask someone there," he suggested. "There must be someone around who can tell you." I explained that all the students were gone and no one is at the little bar and only cars are left.

"NO ONE is here now. Absolutely no one—and no cars are even passing." I figured that everyone was home eating pranzo and enjoying a little *riposino*. That would be the normal routine.

He was very upset, more than I was. I figured I would eventually be able to ask someone who came to get his car. What can I do? Call a taxi? Call the police, or hitchhike?

Just then I said, "Okay Rocco I just noticed that in one of the two seemingly empty cars parked just outside the gate on the other side, someone's head has popped up! I'll run over and see if I can find out where I am!" *He must have been taking a nap*, I thought.

Figure 76. Mary, mother Rita, and Terry in Filippo's garden, c. 1950

Lo and Behold . . .

With Rocco still on the line, I ran over to the driver's side of the dark grey car and, catching a glimpse inside as I ran up, knuckle at the ready, just about to knock on the window, I noticed that the man was not alone! A middle-aged woman with long bleached-blond hair was in the process of slowly getting up from her reclining position. I was horrified and embarrassed as the very angry gentleman rolled down the window, ready to pounce!

I stammered, apologizing profusely for the disturbance, as Rocco listened, still on the phone. The woman smiled at me though and told her companion to calm down "the woman has a problem—and is obviously a foreigner. She needs help." All the while, she smiled at me, a sort of impish, conspiratorial smile between just us women.

He calmed down, but in a totally disgusted manner with an ugly scrunched up scowl. I explained that I had to tell my cousin where I was so he could pick me up, but I had no idea of the location.

"I'm so sorry, " I stammered. He began to explain begrudgingly and I could tell I would have trouble understanding him, considering my now stressed condition, so I asked if he would mind explaining it to my cousin who was on the phone.

The woman encouraged him and smiled at me again and I introduced him to Rocco as I passed the phone. They discussed the location, which seemed to go well. He said goodbye to Rocco and handed me the phone, with a smile now, and I bowed humbly and thanked them both as I turned away and spoke with Rocco. Evidently, I was underneath and behind Caltanissetta's main post office, so he would be there to rescue me shortly. He at that time did not know the circumstances of the couple that we had just interrupted, who in the meantime, had resumed whatever had been happening in the front seat of the car.

I went back to my post across the way, discreetly distant from their car, which had a lovely view of the valley.

End of the Story?

Well, I suppose that should have been the end of the story, the rest a predictable evolution of events. Not exactly . . . I waited at my post. The time was 3:00 in the afternoon: it had been an hour and a half since my arrival at the parking lot. I was relieved and a little unnerved by the previous intrusion, but giggled at my own ability to run into these little adventures whenever I ventured off the beaten track. And my Italian—wow, thank goodness I could speak some Italian!

I waited and waited and began to worry when, after twenty minutes they had not arrived. The couple was still there too, but invisible. No traffic, nothing . . . My phone rang again. It was Rocco.

"Maria," he said, "for the love of God where are you? We are at the main post office and can't see you anywhere." I explained that I was not at the post office but at a parking lot behind it, down the hill from it. I explained that I could see the back of the mammoth yellow building from my position down below. "We're in the middle of the city here, Maria. There's no hill and parking lot behind it. Give me another landmark, a point of reference." So, I looked up at the building on the hill and told him the only thing I could see that might be helpful is an absolutely gigantic mass of relay radio towers, discs, etc. probably for cell phone signals. Other than trees up the side of the hill, the back of the building, and the towers, I could see nothing else.

Figure 77. Touring the necropolis outside Pietraperzia

Promise of Success

Bingo! Rocco said, "I see them!!! But, they are not at the main post office, or there is more than one main post office! I'll find my way there." I reminded him that I would be down back behind, not at the towers or the building. In less than five minutes he and Nina were squealing to a stop opposite me, going down hill. Rocco popped out of the car, leaving it more or less in the middle of the road. He started the discussion from across the way, and then embraced me. I suggested timidly that he pull out of the road and park so I could put my suitcase in the trunk. He did.

Reunion

Just then the couple emerged from their car, both smiling and obviously pleased that my cousins had found me and I would be safe. I introduced them to Rocco and Nina and the guys had a guffawing kind of conversation, while we women exchanged pleasantries. Nina would not let go of me; she was so relieved that I was okay. After a few minutes we all said goodbye and shook hands and the couple split up, each in his/her own car and sped off. We piled into Rocco and Nina's car.

Rocco started the engine and immediately began the sermon about what I should have done: "Always go to the real bus station, Maria. Don't ever let a driver leave you off in the middle of nowhere."

My answer, chuckling, was "Rocco, you believe I will ever do this again?" We all burst out laughing and marveled at how little time it took for me to arrive at my Sicilian home, in the middle of the island, and have an adventure—one that brings some excitement to them all! I knew I would be forgiven, and we would have another memory to add to our already burgeoning storybook.

Pietraperzia – Postscript

I thought the story was over, but not quite ... My husband Tom arrived in Pietraperzia the next day and once he had narrated the details of his flights, airport travails, rental car woes, and trip from Catania Airport to Pietraperzia, he asked me how my journey from Palermo had been. I laughed and answered, "Well, I have another story!" I narrated my experiences of the day before, which I had already been required to do for two or three local family members. Everyone was getting a kick out it and since I was laughing and not crying and complaining, they enjoyed it too.

Anyway, he thought for a split second and, in his usual rational way, trying to be helpful, a bit like Rocco's initial advice, said: "But why didn't you use the GPS on your phone to nail down the location?" He was right of course, and perhaps the next time, I would!

Instead I answered "yes, but then we wouldn't have a story—would we?"

Figure 78. Maria Calogera & Filippo with six of eight children, late 1930s

Figure 79. Five of Tolaro children with spouses, 1958

Reflections: Being Italian-American

While this seems to be my story, it is really the story of many Italian immigrants and also of others in my family affected by the new Sicilian cousins. These are their reflections.

Tom Noyes and his Sicilian Heart

The open-armed welcome Maria Calogera, Mary's grandmother, gave me when I first met her after Mary and I were married in 1970, brought this American son of northern European heritage into the Sicilian-American family. She knew Mary and I loved each other and after minutes she understood I would be a good husband for her granddaughter—and that was enough for all the aunts and uncles too. Years later, in 1989, when letters arrived from the Sicilian family welcoming a visit, I changed all the flight plans for my sons and me at the last minute to arrive in Palermo instead of Rome, to drive an immense white van to Pietraperzia, and to be immersed in two enormous Sicilian families. After a few years and numerous return visits, my Sicilian uncles gave me the greatest honor I have ever received, telling me that I have a Sicilian Heart.

Note: *From the beginning my husband Tom has been my partner in this "journey of the heart." The story would be incomplete without his presence and his support.*

Jim Noyes recalls

I visited Italy as a sixteen-year-old, and what first comes to my mind when I look back to 1989 is the amazing welcome of our Sicilian family—which included an abundance of hugs and kisses, freely flowing wine (quite memorable for a sixteen-year old American male), and the never-ending delicious and abundant food! I quickly learned that the most important words for me to know in Italian were "basta, grazie."

Note: *Our older son has only visited Pietraperzia once. University studies prevented him from returning. Hopefully, one day he will bring his family there and our grandsons, Thomas and Andrew, will meet their young Sicilian cousins. Jim was Maria Calogera's first great-grandchild and I remember making the trip* *from southern California to snowy Vermont in mid-December to introduce them when he was barely four months old. He does not remember her happiness and all the hugs and kisses she showered on him. She would be proud to know that he still insists on using her tomato sauce recipe.*

Philip Noyes

Meeting my relatives and spending time in the town of Pietraperzia was an affirmation of my identity. My maternal family history crystallized with the amazing warmth of our relatives and learning their stories. Thinking of Sicily now often leads me to a cascade of remembered tastes, smells, and sights and to picture my grandfather's strong brown hands, calloused from working soil and machines. I dream of building a brick oven in my backyard near my vegetable garden and finding some seasoned olive wood to try and recreate the best tomato pasta sauce I have ever had, that made by my family in the Sicilian *campagna*.

Note: *Philip is our younger son, with whom I have traveled a number of times to Pietraperzia in particular, and in Italy. For this reason he has been able to forge relationships with many of his Pietrini cousins. He has always reminded me so much of his grandfather Philip and my grandmother's stories of my father as a child. Like his grandfather he has a passion for his family, his garden, and his art.*

Figure 80. Phil, grandmother Rita, and Jim, Pietraperzia, 1989

Melissa Wagoner Olesen

I was not sure what to expect when meeting my family in Pietraperzia. Would I feel a connection to them? Would they to me? In the dozens of faces I would see, hundreds of hugs I would receive, and countless meals I would share over the course of the visit, those questions would be answered a dozen times over. A cousin that looked just like my Uncle Jim, with the same sly smile and raucous laughter. A Zarba cousin that looked so much like my great-grandmother that I could not stop staring. Just a few of the joys I experienced and still reflect upon as I think about the dusty streets of Pietraperzia and the warmth I felt as I walked in my great-grandparents' footsteps.

Note: *Melissa and I traveled together to Pietraperzia—and all around Italy—a number of times when she was a university student. Traveling with my niece, my sister Terry's daughter, whose heart and soul are so intrinsically connected to our family, has been one of life's greatest gifts.*

Figure 81. The two Melissas, Pietraperzia, Sept 2006

Julius Tolaro

Reflections on our visit to Pietraperzia? In 2002? Wow—that was already fifteen years ago. Gee—I was only seventy-five years old back then! I had promised my wife Gloria a trip to Italy and Pietraperzia years earlier. I had no idea what it would hold for us. I believed that relatives still lived there, but wondered if they would accept us, how we would communicate, and would it be a disaster? As it turned out my distant cousin Mary, whom we had found through her writing on the Internet, was expecting to be in Palermo at the same time and therefore we would have an interpreter for our visit. Boy did that solve a mess of problems!

When we finally arrived at the Tolaro home in our rental car, most of the relatives were hanging pretty close in order to meet the "new" Tolaros and see Mary again. It was an unbelievable reunion. They showered us with welcoming embraces and kisses, and loving words in the dialect. That was just the hello.

We entered to marble halls and ornate living room walls, but it was the people, our relatives, who were the prize of the joyous visit. It included a lively family style pranzo to satisfy the hungriest tourist and endless conversation gluing it all together.

With only an hour or two left for the visit, we got down to a serious discussion of the family and how we were all related to each other. Although we know we are connected, no one was able to find the common thread. Upon reflection, visiting the town Pietraperzia was fulfilling, but the warmth of the family reception was unforgettable. Even with the language barrier, an instant bonding took place and remains very strong. We are one family.

Note: *Julius, or Jay as we know him, found my author's name somewhere on the Internet years ago. As it turns out, my father had found his Tolaro family in Cleveland, Ohio decades earlier, and actually met them on at least one of his business trips. My father always searched for Tolaros in the white pages of telephone books in every city he visited. None of us worried much about how we were related—we just knew we were! Introducing both Jay and his wife Gloria to the Pietrini cousins was a pleasure for me.*

Figure 82. Jay and Gloria (center) with Tolaro Family, May 2002

Jeanine Carr recalls her grandmother Tolaro

The image is firmly imprinted in my mind. It was my first Communion in 1959 and while I was wearing a white dress and veil, my relatives were all wearing black. That is because Grandpa Tolaro had died just a few days before. I am not sure if the imprint is still with me because I actually remember the reality or because I have a picture of me with my godmother, Aunt Fran, and my godfather, cousin Phil, on that day.

I was only seven years old when Grandpa Tolaro died so I do not remember him well. But I do remember his tomato plants. Grandpa and grandma lived in a house surrounded in the front by a concrete wall and with a small plot of land. It was filled with tomato plants. To this day, when I smell the leaves of the tomato plant, I think of him and their home.

A few months after Grandpa Tolaro died, grandma came to live with my parents, brother, and me. She lived with us for twenty-one years. She became our second mother who cooked for us, helped us with household chores, hugged us, and sometimes scolded us. In the meantime, she would spend two weeks every summer in Watertown,

Massachusetts, with her daughter Fran and son-in-law Phillip Crosby.

I have many memories of her cooking in our kitchen. I can still see the long links of homemade sausage on the kitchen table, made with the meat that she ground in the meat grinder and then stuffed into the casings that relatives brought with them when they visited from Boston. Her Eggplant Parmesan was legendary and I made sure to have her tell me how she made it so I could write it down and keep it in my recipe box. True to her Sicilian heritage, she included tomatoes in many dishes – pork chops, Swiss chard, green beans, and of course, pizza and her delicious sauce, simply made with garlic, onion, and basil. How fortunate I am that as a young girl, I was afforded the opportunity to live with her and learn from her.

Figure 83. Jeanine with mother Gloria and brother Jim, 1956

Grandma's Eggplant Parmesan

Peel, slice, salt, and then press water out of the eggplant for 1½-2 hours. (Press water out by placing slices on a cutting board, cover them with another cutting board, and weigh down with something heavy.)

Fry slices of eggplant in olive oil until golden.

Layer in an oiled pan: a drizzle of beaten egg, some of the eggplant, then a little tomato sauce, a sprinkle of breadcrumbs, and finally the grated Parmesan cheese.

Repeat the layers ending with breadcrumbs and cheese.

Bake at 350 degrees F. for about 20 minutes.

Note: *Introducing American family to their relatives in Pietraperzia is always a thrill for me. Since Jeanine and I shared much of our childhood in Bellows Falls, our visit to the Pietrini cousins was a very special moment.*

Figure 84. Sunday table at Grandma's, North Walpole, c. 1950s

Figure 85. Fran, Phillip, Kay and Jim, Mom and Dad, c. late 1980s

Figure 86. Melissa giving Zio Rocco gift, September 2006

Matthew Raymond

My Sicilian-American grandmother had one child and died when my father Larry was very young. Her name was Anna—my sister's name—and I know her only through pictures and stories narrated by my father and the few living relatives who knew her. Needless to say, we never shared a meal. We never hugged. And there is so much I want to say to her. I have so many questions.

My wife and I planned a trip to Italy in 2011—one last "drinking vacation" before having our first child. It would be a chance for us to get away before our lives changed dramatically and an opportunity to visit the Sicilian hometown of my great-grandparents.

We booked plane tickets. We took language lessons at the local high school. We connected with distant cousins through Facebook and, with the help of Google Translate, introduced ourselves and said we were coming from Massachusetts. They invited us to their home for dinner.

A year later, together with cousin Mary, we finally met them in person at their home in Pietraperzia. When they opened the door, we knew only enough Italian to greet them, and they enough English to do the same. They kissed our cheeks and we embraced and then we all sat around the huge table and ate pranzo. Later we took a walk around the town and entered Santa Maria Maggiore, the church where my great-grandparents were married. It was a moment I will never forget.

Note: What fun it was to introduce Matthew and his wife Michelle to our family in Pietraperzia. They had prepared themselves well for the encounter and charmed all of their young cousins, who still think of them as the "rock stars" of the family—on both sides of the Atlantic Ocean.

Figure 87. Giacoma, Michelle, Matt and Totò, Pietraperzia, Sept 2011

Meet My Sisters and Brother

My siblings wrote the next three pieces. None of them have ever visited the family in Pietraperzia, but their memories of growing up surrounded by our Sicilian family are ones that they all cherish, just as I do.

Figure 88. Siblings Rita, Mary, Phil and Terry, 2010

Recollections of Terry Tolaro Wagoner

When we were young—I was probably six or seven years old— Dad drove the family to Montreal, Canada, to visit our Sicilian relatives who had immigrated there. We brought along grandma and grandpa Tolaro. I remember that grandpa put a chair in front of the hotel room's door knob to secure it. They had never been in a hotel before! All the cousins spoke French or Italian and there was a lot of food and drink at every meal. On that visit we met Dora and her husband Salvatore and their little son Joseph, as well as Ninetta and her husband Armando. Dora and Ninetta were grandma's nieces, the daughters of her sister Giuseppina.

Years later my husband Bill and I visited Montreal and the family again. I remember that Dora still spoke no English and our two young daughters Melissa and Emily sat there quietly, listening, even though they couldn't understand a word! By that time, Salvatore and Armando were both deceased. Again, my memories of that visit involve the abundance of food and happiness!

Philip Tolaro III Recalls

Dear Grandma and Grandpa,

What a life I have had because of you! Wrapped in the arms of my grandparents, Philip and Maria Calogera, the journey has been full of family love. They found the opportunities for us in art, love of music, and so many family memories of love, comfort, support, and dignity – for all of us children, and for the children of other families too. God bless you. I love you, my grandma, and grandpa.

Rita Tolaro Webb: My Sicilian Origins

My Sicilian heritage fuels my soul. It was the special ingredient in our upbringing, like homegrown tomatoes and basil make up the family spaghetti and meatballs recipe I use today. Although—I am pretty sure the meatballs I have made with elk meat might be a first for our family!

I was too young to remember our life in Bellows Falls because we moved when I was three years old. However, I do remember spending two weeks every other summer with our Sicilian relatives in New England. I have wonderful memories of those visits. My grandmother was in all her glory with her family together again. There was always plenty of laughing, wonderful food, and kissing each of us before we went to bed. Our family and the Sicilian legacy meant a lot to my father. His eyes shined as he related stories of the past and his love for his mother and father, brothers and sisters.

I feel very blessed with my heritage and I know that it is what keeps our family strong and united even today. Oh, and we all do still love the basic Italian pantry staples like tomatoes, olive oil, good cheese, garlic, bread, pasta, and of course wine!

Figure 89. Mary (center back) with mother, siblings and grandparents

Figure 90. Filippo and Maria with six of their eight children, c. 1930

From There to Here—and Back: Family Recipes

What happens to a family recipe when the original sunny Sicilian Mediterranean evolves over the decades and generations in cold, northern New England? I decided to find out. Perhaps looking at the evolution of food traditions reflects the inevitable changes that a family experiences.

My mother Rita, always a loving wife, mother—and daughter-in-law—learned to make my father's favorite dishes, which became staples in our household. Two of them were "Broccoli and Spaghetti" and "Pasta and Beans" (*Pasta Fazool* as I remember hearing it). I liked the former a lot, while it seemed to take longer to acquire a taste for the latter. Except for very American "Boston Baked Beans," beans were not a favorite back then. Since the two recipes translated well from southern Sicilian ingredients to New Hampshire, USA, Maria Calogera replicated them in her unfamiliar northern world.

On a recent visit to Pietraperzia I asked my cousin Damiana Zarba, Zio Rocco's daughter, for the recipes she uses today for "Broccoli and Spaghetti" and "Pasta and Beans." Here they are—and especially the former is just as Maria Calogera repeated in North Walpole and we still use today in our home.

Muzzatura--Pasta with Green Broccoli

By Damiana Zarba

Boil the broccoli in salted water for ten minutes. Drain it, but save the water.
In the same water boil the pasta.
Meanwhile, add olive oil to a frying pan or pot and sauté the garlic. Next add the broccoli to the mixture and sauté lightly. Drain the pasta. One absolutely necessary step is to keep to the side at least a cup of pasta water to add in case more liquid is needed.
Finally, add the drained pasta to the broccoli mixture and sauté a little.
(Serve each portion with grated Pecorino cheese.)

Pasta with Beans and Lentils

By Damiana Zarba

Soak beans overnight with a ½-tsp. of baking soda (Do not soak the lentils.)
Drain the beans and put to the side. Meanwhile sauté some chopped carrots and onions in olive oil. Add a small amount of tomatoes. Allow this mixture to cook a little.
Then add enough water to cover and bring to a boil.
Add beans, lentils, celery, a bay leaf, and a small, dried pepperoncino.
(Serve over cooked pasta with grated Pecorino cheese.)

Rita's Versions of Maria Calogera's Recipes

Here are my mother's versions, in her own words, of grandma's two recipes. She no doubt altered them to suit my opinionated father's tastes. When I use her recipes I often smile and feel her presence in the kitchen because of her familiar voice and style.

Grandma's Broccoli and Spaghetti

Broccoli (We like a lot.)
Spaghetti
2-3 cloves of garlic, diced very small (I usually grate just a little onion too.)
Salt
Black pepper
Olive oil
Cook broccoli in more water than usual, as you want to save it for cooking the spaghetti. Only cook broccoli to half done. Drain it but save the water.
While cooking broccoli, add olive oil to a frying pan (More than you usually use for sautéing). Then add the garlic. (Be careful not to have the oil too hot as garlic burns easily.)
Drain broccoli and sauté in frying pan with the oil and garlic until it is cooked enough to satisfy you. Also add seasonings. Be sure to save the broccoli water, as you need to cook the spaghetti in it.
When spaghetti is cooked, do not drain all of the water out of it. In fact, save a little more if necessary. The oil and water remaining make it moist.
Love,
Mom

Fagioli—Pasta e Fasola

I use ½ pound of beans. Wash a couple of times. Add enough water to cover and soak overnight. You can always add more if necessary.
Drain and cover with water and cook until still firm, but tender. Add salt to taste.
Sauce:
I use about two cups of canned tomatoes, strained. You could use tomato sauce if you wish. Sauté a small onion, chopped, and about two to three cloves of garlic, minced, in about two table-

144

spoons of olive oil. Add tomatoes and one small can of tomato paste. Add sweet basil and dried oregano, or any other herb you like. Simmer until thick, and then add beans and also some of the water as you can always add more later to make a thinner sauce. However, it should be a good red color and a little thicker than the water.

Cook *ditellini* or break spaghetti into short pieces. The *ditellini* come in all sizes, so it is up to you, the size you prefer. Dad likes the medium size.

Strain and add to sauce.

After I place it in a bowl, dad sprinkles crushed red pepper over it.

Your son Phil had it here while he was in Florida.
Love,
Mom

Pasta al Forno—According to Zia Giacoma and Nina Tolaro

I do not remember the following baked pasta dish for Sunday dinner at grandma and grandpa's house. However, on our first visit to Pietraperzia in 1989 we learned that every branch of each family prepared its own version. Tom wrote down this version as I translated and helped Nina and Zia Giacoma prepare it that unforgettable Sunday in 1990. (Later the same day we also encountered the capricious goats on the way to Piazza Amerina.) We were houseguests of those same Tolaros and woke up to find no household water. Evidently, one of the main pipes had broken, leaving everyone in the town without running water. To be honest it seemed like a normal occurrence to everyone except us Americans. Rocco and Totò were already out in the countryside with large containers to retrieve water from the fountain/spring. Of course, bottled water was available for drinking, but all other activities requiring water became more complicated.

Naturally, we Americani wondered if the planned grand family pranzo would still go forward—and it did. Pasta al Forno, wine, bread, roasted chicken, sausages, meatballs, vegetables and salad, fruit and a dessert tray filled with cannoli, and many other unimaginable delicacies, caffè, and a *digestivo* to finish up.

Then came the cleanup. Of course, as one of the women of the family I joined forces in the kitchen and stood back in amazement at the set-up for cleanup. The table had been arranged with basins of water and an assembly line of sorts had been formed, each one of us waiting to play our part:

1.) Rinse off scraped plates in first basin;
2.) Second rinse in clean water;
3.) Wash in warm soapy water;
4.) Rinse in clean water;
5.) Pass cleaned dishes to waiting hands for drying and putting away.

We had a wonderful time, and Tom even broke ranks with the men and joined us. He does not like to miss out on a party. At a certain point I remember commenting to Zia Sarina about the meal, the lack of water, and the persistence—with smiles—of the family. Her response is what I remember every time I face unplanned, problematic circumstances: "Pazienza, cara Maria, pazienza," she sighed. Patience had never been one of my strong points. However, that day I understood the enduring value of patience and time, not to mention the fun of family road trips.

Baked Pasta alla Pietraperzia

Preheat oven to 350 degrees F.
Prepare two tomato sauces, one thicker than the other.
Cook hard-boiled eggs to slice or crumble.
Sauté chopped onions in olive oil and add peas.
Prepare prosciutto, crudo or cooked (slices or chopped, according to preference.)
Prepare mozzarella cheese, either sliced or shredded.
Grate Parmesan or Pecorino Romano cheese.

Cook large pasta, i.e. rigatoni, leaving it extra *al dente*.
In the bottom of an oiled baking dish, spread a little beaten egg and enough of the thick sauce to cover the bottom.
Mix thinner sauce into the cooked pasta.
Add a layer of sauced pasta to the baking dish.

Sprinkle half of the peas and prosciutto, eggs, mozzarella cheese, and grated cheese.

Repeat all the layers.

Add tomato sauce if necessary.

Cover tightly with aluminum foil.

Bake at 350 degrees F. for about thirty-five minutes or until heated through. Remove foil and spread on top a light layer of beaten egg, grated cheese and little olive oil.

Bake for another twenty to thirty minutes until top is lightly browned. Let rest for at least ten minutes before cutting into squares and serving.

Can also be made with rice. Both versions are wonderful baked in a wood oven.

Figure 91. Maria Calogera, preparing to can - something - early 1950s

In the Kitchen with Grandma

When I recollect private times with my grandmother Maria Calogera, the kitchen often comes to mind first. Even today at times I can hear her voice saying to me "Now Mary Alice . . ."

Private moments with my grandma often took place in her kitchen, helping with dishes, setting the table, preparing fresh vegetables from grandpa's garden, or just talking, with her giving me kitchen lessons. She taught me the proper way to dry dishes, for instance.

"Mary Alice, you should dry a dish holding it with one part of the clean dishtowel while wiping carefully with the other," she demonstrated. Grandma would have been standing in front of the old kitchen sink, the faded full apron covering her cotton housedress, as she looked at me. I would wipe the dish carefully with the red and white checked towel and carry it to the pantry for her to put away later.

Another moment I never forget is her admonishment to rinse every last speck of tomato sauce from the big pot (or from the can) with a little water and combine it with the leftover sauce to be stored in the refrigerator. I still do it and think of her every time. (My husband Tom does the same.) She never wanted to waste any food, especially anything related to tomatoes.

Canning tomatoes in her kitchen was a summertime ritual with bushels of the vine-ripened, juicy fruit and glistening canning jars at the ready. Eventually I was old enough to help and my job, along with my sister Terry's, was to peel the tomatoes that had been plopped into the very hot water and then to strip off the peel, remove the core and any bad spots, and to toss them into a huge pot to be heated before being placed in the jars. The job was hot and tedious in the humidity of late summer days in southern New Hampshire, but the experience of working together with my mother and grandmother, aunts, sister, and cousins turned it into a pleasant yearly ritual.

Canning pole beans and yellow-waxed beans fresh from the garden, picking Swiss chard, spinach, zucchini squash, and eggplant out in the garden are vivid memories as well. My little sister, brother and I loved playing in the garden's rich dirt with our pails and shovels much to my grandfather's chagrin. Poor grandma always tried to cover up our footprints and fill in the evidence of our digging before he arrived home from work. Most of the time she was successful, but we heard about it from grandpa when she was not.

When she was making bread, she would give me a piece of dough to work myself and create my own miniature loaf. Playing with dough was fun and eating my own "loaf" of bread even more so. Her container for letting the bread dough rise was a huge stainless steel soup or pasta pot covered with a dishtowel. Her bread days would have been very busy when she made bread for the family of ten. She always bragged though that she was the first one in the neighborhood to have a beautiful new electric stove because grandpa looked after her.

Figure 92. Maria Calogera's bread pans with Mary's bread, 2015

My mother, Rita, made bread as well and inherited her mother-in-law's loaf pans, which I now use in my own kitchen. Oh, the wonderful smells that emanate in a kitchen where the magic of bread being lovingly kneaded and baked is unparalleled! It began for me in grandma's kitchen.

In 2014 my husband and I spent much of Holy Week including

Easter in Pietraperzia and a bread story emerged as well. When I participated at a meeting of organizers in Pietraperzia I discovered that grandma's *cudduruni* endeared me not only to my Pietrini family but also to the gathering. The cultural group was focused on their food specialties and had asked me if my grandparents had ever prepared them. I mentioned *cudduruni* and the assembly erupted with pleasure and applause—mostly because I used the Sicilian word.

My father had always looked forward to eating it when my mother, following in my grandmother's footsteps, made bread dough. We would have fried bread dough for Sunday breakfast after Mass. Once the dough had been rolled out flat, perhaps ¾-inch thick, it was cut into pieces, roughly 3-inches square and each one deep fried in hot vegetable oil, then drained. Each was pried open with a fork, spread with butter and drizzled with Vermont maple syrup. Maple syrup was the American answer to the warm bread being dredged in granulated sugar or spread with honey—or perhaps eaten warm with olive oil and cheese.

Dad always requested his mother's version of *cudduruni*. She would roll out a portion of bread dough about the size of a grapefruit until it was about ½-inch thick. Next abundant olive oil was splashed over the surface and salt and plenty of black pepper sprinkled on top. The flattened dough was rolled, jellyroll style, and then wrapped around itself into a flat round shape, resembling an American cinnamon roll. The dough was fried until golden brown. Once drained and slightly cooled, Dad would break the *cudduruni* into bite-sized pieces and put them in a cereal bowl of warm coffee-flavored milk and dig in with a soup spoon. I realized after my meeting in Pietraperzia that not only every town has its typical version of *cudduruni*, but even every family.

While mulling over kitchen memories at grandma's house another came to mind. We always called the pastries "ravioli," but I discovered they are often referred to as *cassateddi* in Sicilian (*cassatelli* in Italian). Making them at Eastertime was our tradition and a great family endeavor, children included. What I remember the best was my job brushing the warm baked pastry raviolis filled with sweetened ricotta cheese and coated with honey after they had cooled a little. When Aunt Gloria and I recently looked back at our family tradition and the fun we had had, she reminded me of the multicolored sprinkles that finished off the delicacy and that sometimes we covered the *cassateddi* with granulated sugar instead of honey—decorated with sprinkles of course.

Vis-à-vis pastry and desserts, grandma was encouraged to make apple pies by her first-born daughter Mary, who pined to bring America into their kitchen. The autumn wild apples were plentiful in New Hampshire and gathered by the children up behind the house on the rugged hill. Maria Calogera did not have any traditional American pie plates at the beginning, which evidently did not pose a problem: each child had a personal apple pie baked in an ovenproof deep dinner plate. My father never ceased to marvel at those apples pies of his youth. I remembered this when I first made apple pies for my friend Clara's family in Bologna in 1996. In fact, large, ovenproof dinner plates do work very well.

Life in the kitchen—often our childhood memories become a family's language of the heart.

Figure 93. Damiana and friends making the *cudduruni*, 2007

Figure 94. Zio Rocco's family, c. 1970s

Figure 95. American family at Aunt Gloria's 50th wedding anniversary

Family Stories

Every family has stories that become favorites. Mine often refer to growing up with the Sicilian-American family in a small New England village. However, my life is doubly blessed with other stories from both my American and Sicilian relatives.

According to Aunt Gloria . . .

Aunt Gloria, my father's only living sibling, and her husband Uncle Jim Carr have always been an important part of my life. When we were children our families lived in the same neighborhood of "King's Field" in Bellows Falls. We spent as much time at their house as at our own. Cousins Jeanine and Jim Carr were our constant playmates. Two memories always come to mind when I think of them. For some reason we often ate Saturday lunch at their house and Aunt Gloria made (and still does make) the best Boston Baked Beans in the world, and blueberry muffins and pie and scones and Pepper Hash relish and Bread and Butter pickles and I will stop there. In summertime they would load the three of us (sister Rita was not yet born) in their green 1950s Ford sedan and take us to a swimming hole somewhere in the area. Uncle Jim would bring their little grill and we would roast hot dogs and marshmallows and swim and argue too. Luckily, they were very patient.

Recently Tom and I were able to have a lovely visit with them in Bellows Falls and remember those times. They are both in their nineties and exchanged many memories as we sat on the screened in back porch on the warm summer afternoon.

According to Aunt Gloria, grandpa grew "fields" of tomatoes and grandma canned them. He created a robust garden that encircled their house and even went up the hill behind it. I too remember tall thin tree limbs stuck in the ground with pole beans climbing up them. They also surrounded grandma's one beautiful rose trellis. Besides tomatoes he grew many varieties of greens: spinach, endive, escarole and Swiss chard, especially Swiss chard! Likewise he cultivated zucchini squash and yellow summer squash, eggplants, and bushes of yellow beans.

We also remembered my favorite garden story, which concerns

the fig tree he tended on the side of the hill. Every autumn the big discussion would be how to keep it alive over the winter. Once he built a little house around it. He used old wood framed windows for the sides and even had a shingled roof on top so the snow would slide off. I asked him if he would build us a playhouse in the summertime, but he never did. Land was for cultivating food, not for playing dolls—or for growing flowers either!

Aunt Gloria recounted a memory that emphasizes the quantity of food her father grew to feed their eight children (and us too when we were growing up) and how hard grandma worked, not only in the house but in the garden as well. Evidently, they had not only the garden that circumscribed their house, but also a field of crops about a mile and a half away, above the Connecticut River. She described walking there with her mother as a young girl, each carrying a pail. They would go down to the river and haul buckets of river water up to feed the plants one by one. She marvels that they did not drown as they plunged their pails into the rushing water!

She also reinforced my memory of how much Filippo loved Maria and constantly demonstrated his affection. A very impatient man, he showed his vulnerability by the way he treated her.

Another previously unknown anecdote illustrates how difficult their life in the New World was in 1913. Since grandpa worked for the Boston and Maine Railroad they lived in what seems to have been an extremely rustic, isolated cottage in the area of Westmoreland, New Hampshire, where a depot and little else existed. The house had no insulation and I too remember grandma talking about filling in cracks and covering windows with newspaper to block the frigid drafts in the wintertime. However, the new image I have is the one related by Aunt Gloria, as told by her mother. Grandma described washing clothes by hand and hanging them to dry in the wintertime, wet clothes that became as hard as boards as they dried and needed to thaw out to be worn. Then too, after washing the floor, grandma, the young Sicilian bride, literally "skated" across the icy surface inside the house. Life was not easy for those who chose to emigrate.

When it came to her older brother, my father, Aunt Gloria also had a couple of stories to share. Dad always had a candy stash, usually chocolate. Evidently, he would remunerate his younger sister with a piece of chocolate, or twenty-five cents if she would polish his shoes or wash his hair for him, including a lovely head massage of course! Big brothers . . .

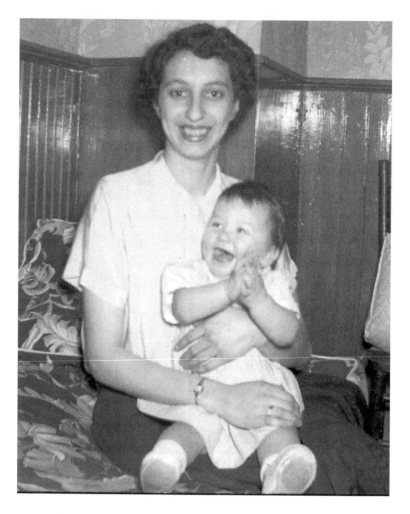

Figure 96. Aunt Gloria with cousin Jeanine, early 1950s

Then Uncle Jim chimed in about shopping trips with my grandfather, whose habits were strictly "old country" barter and trade style. For instance grandpa would call him and say " I need go to Boston for wine" and Uncle Jim would take him. They would go to the North End and I can see it now, grandpa in his black and red checkered jacket and Sunday fedora and Uncle Jim patiently following along. They would start at one establishment and ask a price and grandpa would insist that it was too high. They would move down the street, always with the same result. In the end, after a few hours of negotiations and bluster, they would return to the first seller for the purchase of his wine. The same story unfolded when he needed shoes: a call to Uncle Jim, a ride to Keene, NH, and a day-long search for a pair of shoes, which could have been purchased at the initial locale. Barter and trade, otherwise, shopping is no fun and certainly a swindle. Uncle Jim described those excursions with a twinkle in his eye and a lovely sweet smirk on his very taciturn Vermont countenance. Despite my grandfather's demands, he remembers him with fondness and a chuckle.

According to Aunt Gloria, life was very difficult but filled with the love that I too remember as I grew up in my immigrant family's embrace.

Pirzisi Gets Around

On a lovely June day in 1989 at the Villa Romana just outside of Piazza Amerina my father was unexpectedly welcomed "home." He, my mother, and I had been on a tour of Southern Italy and Sicily with my Italian teacher as the guide and the tour bus had already passed by the Enna and Pietraperzia road signs triggering o-o-h's and a-a-h's and shivers of anticipation. We would soon be leaving the group and heading out on our own to meet the family. Our thoughtful guide Bruna, who had taken an interest in our story and especially my father's enthusiasm, had been encouraging him to speak Italian or the family dialect throughout the journey but he shied away and said, "No, I never learned the language. We were always required to speak English at home. My parents wanted us to be American!"

That day at the Villa, however, Bruna tried again. Our group had stopped just outside the ruins at the makeshift coffee bar that provided a couple of umbrella tables and folding chairs for its clients. Around one table a jolly group of elderly signori were conversing and our outgoing guide approached them to chat while the rest of us occupied the other table. After a few minutes she called "Phil, come over here. I want you to meet some friendly gentlemen!" My father and I went over to join her and the group and they encouraged him to say hello and tell them something about his family. He did, and totally surprised himself because the words and phrases came out in the ancient *pirzisi* dialect, the one he had heard his parents use when speaking to each other. All in a chorus the men exclaimed, "Your family is from Pietraperzia! We can tell from how you speak."

My father was shocked. He actually could speak the dialect—and the gentlemen could recognize the town by its dialect. After that he was less shy and, when we finally arrived in Pietraperzia, satisfying conversations were possible with his uncle, Zio Rocco, and the other Tolaro and Zarba family members. Therefore, Piazza Armerina and the Villa Romana remain special to us. *Pirzisi* gets around.

Figure 97. Bruna, with us the night before going to Pietraperzia, 1989

Figure 98. Maria Calogera with grandchildren Jeanine, Phil, and Larry

Figure 99. Zia Concetta and Rita Tolaro, 1989

Giggles and Grandmothers

At the canter of a make-believe horse I would sing to Viviana, our firstborn granddaughter, "Mana—manuzza—le. A—saw—la— we—je—le. A—tatta—ta-ta. A—tatta—ta-ta. Wee ... wee!" Giggles ... belly giggles all around! Viviana would giggle just like I used to when my grandmother Maria Calogera put me on her lap facing her and, holding my two little hands, she raised and lowered the heels of both feet in unison while singing the nursery rhyme. Her lap with me on it would raise and lower, jostling me pleasantly. The words did not truly matter, and perhaps why only a vague memory of them lingers. What did matter was the staccato rhythm of a cantering horse on grandma's lap and her smiling eyes focused only on me—and the finish, of course: Giving slack to the reins and dipping me back gently, twice—and thus the two *whees* at the end of my moment with Viviana. Two times. Two dips. What a thrill it was! And what giggles followed ...

Here are the words to the rhyme in *pirzisi*, given to me by my cousin Nina Tolaro-Pagliaro. Yes, we grandmothers still bounce our giggling grandchildren just so on our dancing laps, and finish of course, with a perfect hug.

Manu manuzza lè,
Passà lu vice rè.
Purtà li cosi nova,
Casca cascavaddu friutu cu l'ova!

The Old Mouse and the Little Mouse

Once upon a time there were two little boys named Philip ... one was my father, the other my son. Grandma used to tell me stories about her children growing up. Eight children would provide enumerable stories for anyone. One of my favorites about my father, her fourth child and third son, dealt with the subject of chocolate and mice. Evidently, little Philip was crazy about chocolate candy and no matter how high grandma hid the treat he would find it and enjoy a nibble or two. She always knew Philip did it although she never caught him and compared him to a sneaky mouse. Growing up, we children always knew our father had a chocolate drawer, well within reach, but we were not allowed to ever help ourselves. Dad was generous, however, and I always thought of him as grandma's "little mouse."

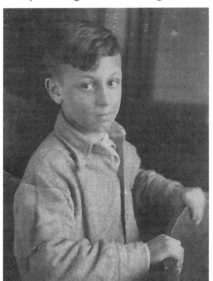 

Figure 100. Old Mouse and Little Mouse, author's father and son

We have a son named Philip too, after his grandfather and great-grandfather and guess what? He likes chocolate! When he was a child we had a root cellar in our Michigan house where we stored chocolate bars, along with fruits and vegetables. One day when our little Philip was probably five or six years old I noticed that the chocolate bars had nibbles out of them and immediately thought of mice. Mice had previously gotten into some of the dried beans and root vegetables in the past, so my immediate reaction was to blame a chocolate-loving mouse. However, when I brought the bars into the daylight and looked more closely, I realized that the tooth-marks were definitely human and not those of a mouse. Our "little mouse" also happened to be a Philip.

Later on I remarked to my father with a chuckle that his namesake grandchild certainly took after him—he too was a "little mouse." My father laughed, but added, "No, according to grandma I was 'the Old Mouse,' since I never got caught!"

Sisters — Maria Calogera and Giuseppina

I recently came into possession of a package of old photographs and notes, primarily the one-sided correspondence received over the years by Maria Calogera from her sister Giuseppina. I met Zia Giuseppina at least two times, when she visited her children Dora, Ninetta, and Enzo, who were living in Montreal, Canada. Somewhere in my memory I believe my grandmother, along with our family, made a road trip from Bellows Falls to Montreal to visit the Canadian cousins before Zia Giuseppina's return to Pietraperzia. Therefore, grandma and her sister probably met face to face twice over the decades. As a child of perhaps ten years old two episodes come to mind. One took place in Vermont and the other in Montreal. Grandma was happy and nervous about the encounters. She had been separated from her family for about forty or more years. When the Canadian family visited I remember being overwhelmed by how handsome Enzo Lo Manto was and by his voice. He was a "famous" Canadian crooner of Italian standards and I accompanied him on the piano while he sang *O Sole Mio*! That was in the day of Perry Como, Dean Martin, and Frank Sinatra . . . Although my hands were shaking I did it! I was so proud—and imagine he had never recalled the experience.

The other episode is that of grandma asking Zia Giuseppina where the bathroom was when we were in Montreal. She thought she was asking in the dialect but the word she used was *baccaousa*. In reality she was asking in a pigeon form of English/Sicilian for the back house and no one understood. She had always been adamant about speaking only English at home. Eventually her English merged with the *pirzisi*.

One final note of commentary: All my Pietrini Zarba cousins speak of Zia Giuseppina as a wonderfully warm, caring person, who showered love and affection on them all. In reading the notes she wrote to her sister Maria Calogera over the years, I have no doubt that they are correct. Her frequent affectionate correspondence continues to bring tears to my eyes whenever I read the notes. Sisters forever.

Figure 101. Giuseppina and Maria Calogera, Bellows Falls, c. 1970

Figure 102. Cettina with husband Angelo and mother Damiana, 1992

Figure 103. Mary with Tom presenting Italian book in San Francisco

And Granddaughters Who Write

The following poem is in Sicilian, written by my second cousin, Concetta Bifarella, grandaughter of Giuseppina. An unpublished poet, she wrote poignant poetry in *pirzisi*, Pietraperzia's dialect, and shared them with me. The theme of the following poem is one hundred poems and their manifestations all around us—love, patience, goodness. Life is short and we must appreciate it.

Cintu Poesia

Cintu cci nni vunu poesia
cintu ppi decantari a tia,
ppi tuttu l'amuri ca nti lu pettu purti
cintu, lunghi lunghi, e nun certu curti.

Cintu ppi la bonta' e li boni modi
n'antri cintu ppi decantari li lodi.
Cintu ppi tutta l'infinita to pazienza,
n'antri cintu ppi mostrariti la ma benevolenza.

Ppi diriti l'amuri ca ti purtu,
lu timpu di la vita ie' troppo curtu.
E ci vunu ancora nantri cintu poesia,
ppi ringraziari De' ca appartini a mia.

Figure 104. Salvatore Zarba at work, c. 1950s

Figure 105. Zio Rocco, in procession, c. 1940s

The Zarba Family Cart Drivers

A number of years ago Zio Rocco made it very clear that the life of the Zarba family cart drivers had not been a glamorous one. He was about to be Grand Marshall in the evocative procession of beautifully restored, colorful Sicilian carts to the Sanctuary of the Madonna della Cava. I had known the history of the Zarba family—that my great-grandfather Vincenzo had driven a *carretto*, and his sons as well. As an American my image was the result of watching movies, with happy families trundling off to the countryside for a picnic and singing and dancing. Instead, the life of the *carrettiere* was one of long days traversing rocky, narrow, rutted roads with a hard-working mule as a companion. As Zio Rocco had admonished me on that day: "Maria," he said, "We did not have dashing white horses with colorful feather plumes. Our cart was drawn by a mule."

His son Vincenzo, named after his grandfather, kept the family *carretto* in the garage. On an early visit to the town he and my father had rolled it out into the street and posed for a photo. Vincenzo like his father could not part with it—he too had been a *carrettiere* while growing up.

Meanwhile, great-grandfather Vincenzo's other son Salvatore had carried on the family tradition as well. In 2016 my husband Tom and I sat down with Salvatore's son, another Vincenzo, and asked him about his life as a *carrettiere*. "We worked long hours," he said, "in all kinds of weather and every day, if we had to." He added that normally they transported gypsum to Catania, excavated from the surrounding rocky hills. They also carried fruits, vegetables, and grain grown in the fields, and passengers—often prisoners—back and forth.

"Prisoners?" I asked, surprised by the information. Evidently the castle up on the crest of the hill had once been converted to a prison; thus the need for transporting them to and from the surrounding towns and cities. "So that's why grandma never mentioned a castle when she had described Pietraperzia to me! When she was growing up, it had been a prison that overlooked the town."

And then we studied Vincenzo's old photos, featuring the family's *carretto* of course, sometimes crowded with family members on the way to a picnic in the countryside.

Figure 106. Vincenzo Zarba (di Salvatore) with family, c. 1950

Women in Black

Grandma would not wear the color black, even when my grandfather or one of her children died. I remember my elders' discussions when the necessity arose. This attitude of hers came to mind at our arrival in Pietraperzia in 1989, or in any of the other towns we visited. Especially the older women wore black dresses, casting a somber atmosphere to the place as we walked along the streets. When in mourning, navy blue became grandma's color, her submission to the norm. Women in Black: my Americanized Sicilian grandmother would have none of it.

Maria Calogera's favorite color was in fact, light blue, the color of her eyes. When she dressed up in a light blue outfit, complete with a matching hat, she seemed so proud and walked like the queen my grandfather always called her.

Figure 107. Maria Calogera in Royal Blue, Michigan, 1970s

Figure 108. Vincenzo Zarba and Family, May 1995

Figure 109. Pittiniddu

Pittiniddu – All About the Hair

I automatically think of my father Philip as the American "Pittiniddu." However, his brothers James and Michael could very well have carried the Zarba nickname too. They were all blessed with the most beautiful, thick, wavy black hair, which eventually morphed into beautiful, wavy and silvery white before their deaths. Growing up I had heard the story of the nickname given to my great-grandfather Vincenzo Zarba. Evidently he had beautiful, thick, wavy hair and carried a pocket comb, which he used frequently to call attention to its magnificence. Thus, the nickname "Pittiniddu," a Sicilian word derived from *pittinari*, to comb, in this case the hair.

Many male Pietrini cousins claim the same gorgeous attributes as my American father and uncles. In fact, when I am in Pietraperzia and an acquaintance asks which branch of the Zarba family I belong to, I proudly respond: "Sono di Pittiniddu (I belong to the Zarba Pittiniddu family!)" And it all becomes very clear ...

Family

Vincenzo Zarba is a quiet and thoughtful man. Recently he explained to me that his father Salvatore could never forgive his sister Maria Calogera for leaving Pietraperzia and believed, because she had never returned, that she must not have loved them and had wanted to forget the family. I was able to describe my grandparents' difficult life—the poverty, the hard work, and the isolation they faced. "I'm here because of my grandparents' love for their families and Pietraperzia," I assured him. "Your American family returned on their behalf because of what they gave us—the desire to come here and reunite the family." My cousin Vincenzo just barely smiled and nodded "yes, now I understand." When we left he embraced me and whispered "Ti voglio bene, Maria." (I love you, Mary.) A moment I cherish and will never forget.

Figure 110. Climb to the Castle

Epilogue

Our first meeting in 1989 was like a dream, with the reality of Italy and my Sicilian family replacing the images of the past. Real people with names and faces and histories replaced the characters in the stories I had heard and imagined. A real town with streets my grandparents had known replaced the fairytale town of my memories. I saw the balcony on which Filippo had first glimpsed Maria Calogera and fallen in love with her. Real experiences linked me to cousins anxious to know about the life of my grandparents and their family in the United States.

Then the passion flamed. Perhaps nothing, other than recognizing my husband Tom as my soul mate, has determined my life as deeply as my first visit to Pietraperzia.

Since then, I have studied the language, history, culture, written letters unceasingly to family and friends that I have made, and returned innumerable times.

What does Italy and being Italian-American mean to me now? I do not know the final answer. I only know that I am learning. It is a process. What began as a journey to understand my grandmother better has exploded into a journey of self-discovery. I have lived there often for months at a time, studying, absorbing, and growing as a person and in my love for the way of life and the people. My relationship with the country and the traditions does not revolve only around the family that I have found and who has truly embraced me. Somehow, in a way I do not fully comprehend—Italy is united intrinsically to the person I am and continue to discover each time I return.

Italy is real to me, personal, home, with problems I have witnessed and aspects I sometimes do not understand. It is the people I have met, the acceptance I have felt, the day-to-day life revolving around relationships that I have experienced, the language that I am learning. It is the first real conversation I had with my dear Zio Rocco. It is the friends who insisted I spend my final few days with them so I would not be alone before my trip home to California one November. In Italy I have realized the world that comforts my soul, quickens my passion, and inspires my life.

My grandmother Maria Calogera and my father Philip helped show the way. And the heart's inspiring journey continues ...

Figure 111. Dad holding soil from the land his father purchased in 1913

Table of Images